socialist
alternative

This work was published by Red Flag books, an imprint of
Socialist Alternative, Australia's largest revolutionary socialist group.

Find out more about Socialist Alternative, read our fortnightly
newspaper, and browse our bookstore at *redflag.org.au*

This edition published by Red Flag Books
Melbourne, March 2025

Red Flag Books is an imprint of Socialist Alternative
redflag.org.au

Cover design by James Plested
Interior Layout by Luka Kiernan

Printed by IngramSpark

From little things big things grow:

Strategies for building revolutionary socialist organisations

MICK ARMSTRONG

R

**RED FLAG
BOOKS**

Table of contents

Introduction

Relentless austerity, never ending wars, union busting, multi-million dollar executive salaries, Muslim bashing, environmental destruction and draconian police powers – welcome to twenty-first century capitalism.

For over three decades workers in virtually every advanced capitalist country have faced an unrelenting offensive against their working conditions, their right to organise and their basic public services – health care, education and social welfare. This assault has been backed up by an ideological offensive aimed at undermining many of the core social gains won in the last great upsurge of radicalism in the 1960s and 1970s. There has been a concerted attempt to reimpose "family" values. Refugees and Muslims have been demonised. Aboriginal people pilloried and democratic rights severely undermined. The dog-eat-dog values of free market neoliberalism are today upheld as sacrosanct. And on top of all this our rulers' "war on terror" has delivered decade after decade of murderous war.

The case for a different type of society – a socialist society where human need, not corporate profit, is the criterion on which the vital decisions that affect our lives are made, and where mass democracy replaces the rule of a tiny band of multi-billionaires – could not be more compelling. Yet the Labor Party that traditionally claimed to defend working class interests long ago embraced the neo-liberal agenda. Indeed under Hawke and Keating the ALP played a path breaking role in imposing privatisation and attacks on living standards. As official politics has moved to the right, a growing gulf has opened up between the hopes and aspirations of millions of working people and the agenda of the ruling capitalist establishment and its parties, both Liberal and Labor.[1]

Internationally this discontent has fuelled increasing political polarisation. On the one hand there has been the growth of far right and fascist organisations such as Marine Le Pen's National Front in France, the election of Donald Trump in the US, the election for the first time since World War II of Nazis to the German parliament and the re-emergence of Pauline Hanson here in Australia. On the other hand in some countries it has been the left that has benefited from the discontent with the widespread support for Bernie Sanders in the US, the rise of the left winger Jeremy Corbyn to the leadership of the British Labour party, the election of Syriza in Greece, the emergence of Podemos in Spain.

Over the last two decades in Australia the disenchantment and discontent for most of the time has found no outlet, but then it explodes in massive mobilisations like those against the outbreak of the Iraq war in 2003 or WorkChoices in 2005/2006. These upheavals had the potential to turn the political tide, to end the assault on our living standards and put the bosses and their governments on the back foot. The tragedy is that because of the failure of the trade union leaders, the ALP and Greens to lead on-going resistance, the potential of those mobilisations was repeatedly squandered. The confidence and hopes of millions for a better world were briefly raised. In the campaign against WorkChoices workers gained a sense of their collective power. But the abject failure of the union leadership meant that the momentum was not sustained. Defeat was clutched from the jaws of victory. As a consequences hope faltered. Confidence receded. It seemed that there was no alternative to our rulers' neo-liberal agenda.

There is a burning need for a socialist alternative that will harness that discontent on an ongoing basis so that sustained rank and file organisations are built in the workplaces and campuses, fighting democratic movements are cohered, and confidence-building victories are chalked up. If a socialist party had existed with even five or ten thousand members, it could have cohered an ongoing movement against the Iraq war that would have put the Howard government on the defensive. A socialist party with hundreds of student activists could have challenged the do nothing ALP-aligned leadership of the National Union of Students and helped sustain a movement that defeated the Liberals' union busting Voluntary Student Union legislation. A socialist party with some implan-tation in the working class – one or two thousand delegates and shop stewards – could have made a decisive difference to the campaign against WorkChoices. It would have been in a position to lead industrial action that could have turned Howard's laws into a dead letter.

But if the case for building a genuine socialist party is clear, this urgent task still very much remains in front of us. How do we go about building such a party from small groups of socialists? Where do we start? On what political basis should we organise? Where should we concentrate our activity? How should we relate to other forces on the left? Indeed, is it possible to build such a party? This short book aims to address these questions and many more. It does not claim to have all the answers, not by any means. Many of the answers can only be worked out in the course of actively building such a party in the battles of the future.

Nonetheless, the experience of the Marxist movement over the last 160 years or more does offer us some important guidelines. Today's revolutionaries are not the first to embark on the project of trying to build from scratch a party that can lead the working class to power. We can draw vital lessons from the successes and failures of those dedicated fighters for working class emancipation that have gone before us. They have laid down a tradition upon which we can build. An important aspect of this book is a series of case studies of how revolutionary socialists have built in a wide range of different circumstances in the past. But it is not just the lessons and traditions of the past that we can draw on; we in Socialist Alternative believe that we have gained some important insights from our own activity in building a socialist organisation in Australia over the last two decades. Hopefully this short book will play some role in politically arming a new generation of socialist activists to take up the fight for a better world. If it helps stimulate debate and discussion on these vital questions it will have served its purpose.

CHAPTER ONE

The nature and tasks of a socialist propaganda group

The aim of Marxists is to build a mass revolutionary party that can cohere working class resistance to the attacks of the capitalist class and eventually lead a revolution that will bring workers to power. But the reality is that in every country socialists are currently a very long way from achieving that goal. There are today no mass revolutionary parties and a genuine revolutionary party is not going to be conjured from thin air. There are no short cuts, no magic formulas. It is going to take determined effort by serious-minded socialists. But the previous history of the socialist movement does provide us with some important guidelines as to how to approach the task.

All the history of our movement shows that socialists can't build a mass revolutionary workers' party until two essential preconditions are met. The first is a decisive radicalisation among a significant layer of workers that makes them receptive to revolutionary ideas. This is almost completely beyond the control of small groups of socialists; it will occur as workers are forced to rebel against the deprivations of world capitalism. The second precondition – one socialists do have some control over – is that we have cohered a reasonably sizeable body of committed revolutionaries, a cadre, that is capable of intervening in mass struggles with convincing arguments to win a layer of workers to socialism. The traditional mechanism by which that initial cadre is cohered is via a socialist propaganda group.

In the Marxist tradition there are three main types of organisation: discussion circles, propaganda groups and parties. These categories are not arbitrary, but are used to describe qualitatively different types of organisation. Discussion circles are tiny groups attempting to establish a Marxist tradition. Their main orientation is theoretical clarification. Political activity such as selling a paper or intervening in strikes or campaigns is a low priority. They recruit on the basis of a relatively high level of theory. Propaganda groups

are involved in a broader range of activity, but because they are small and lack influence in the working class, they primarily recruit on the basis of ideas.

Socialists make a distinction between two kinds of propaganda: general (sometimes called abstract) and concrete. Discussion circles are mostly concerned with general propaganda arguing the core ideas of Marxism or the distinctive ideas of a specific revolutionary current. But a propaganda group also engages in concrete propaganda. By this Marxists mean propaganda that might at times seem agitational, i.e. calling for action. For example, socialists called for mass protests to free the refugees on Manus Island and Nauru. A small socialist group could not organise the type of mass action needed to force the government to bring the refugees to Australia and grant them asylum. But by raising the slogan, socialists attempted to find an audience among people who opposed the Australian government's horrific treatment of asylum seekers. Socialists use the specific facts about an issue like the brutal treatment of refugees to build up an argument to convince their audience of the need for open borders and an end to a system that terrorises people fleeing oppression.

In contrast, general propaganda begins from a central proposition of, say, Marxist internationalism and gives a more theorised argument about why someone should for example oppose Australian support for Trump's war drive against North Korea. It should be clear from these examples that there is not always a clear dividing line between concrete and general propaganda. A propaganda group uses both, and while involved in activity, it cannot recruit primarily by demonstrating its politics in action.

A mass party is different again. Because of its weight of numbers and influence, it can have an impact on the class struggle and recruit on this basis. Propaganda is still vital for a party, but the balance of its work may be more agitational. It can, at least for some section of the working class, provide a real alternative to the betrayals of the Labor Party and the reformist trade union leaders and deliver action – it can take struggles forward. In Australia we are talking of a party of tens of thousands.

Discussion circles were important when revolutionaries had to lay down the basic ideas of Marxism. They are still necessary in countries where there is little tradition of Marxism. But once a core of people have settled on the ideas around which they organise, they can begin to think how they can recruit more systematically, while gaining some experience in applying these ideas to the concrete questions and struggles of the day. This entails producing and distributing a regular publication and holding meetings to which people who are not necessarily committed to the core ideas of socialism can come and discuss politics and theory. You then have the basics of a propaganda group.

It is very important to be clear on the distinction between a propaganda group and a mass party – in particular, that propaganda groups do not have the capacity to lead workers in major struggles and recruit on that basis. They must rely primarily on their general socialist ideas. Socialists want to change the world. We would much prefer to be leading mass strikes and demonstrations rather than patiently seeking individual sympathisers. However, we recognise that while we can play an important role in initiating some localised struggles and protests and provide some of the key activists in a variety of campaign groups, we are, as yet, too small to have any serious impact on the major struggles that break out. We can only recruit handfuls of people, not move the masses.

Today Socialist Alternative is in the business of arguing general socialist ideas around a broad range of questions – the nature of imperialism, the need for mass action rather than reliance on parliament, the central role of the working class in fighting for a better world, the difference between genuine socialism and Stalinism – not *organising* mass action, taking over the leadership of the ACTU or offering a serious electoral alternative to the ALP and Greens. Indeed, if we were to attempt to do these things, we would be courting disaster.

If we look at the history of the socialist movement, we can see that one of the key reasons why so many small revolutionary groups came to grief is that they overestimated their own capabilities and greatly exaggerated their ability to influence struggles or campaigns. All too often they attempted to leap over the stage of development dictated by the balance of forces between bosses and workers and the limitations imposed by their own small size. They were too impatient. They often spurned the conception of being a propaganda group and tried to act as "agitational groups". They put out papers with heaps of strike reports, as though they had a mass working class readership. But headlines that don't move workers into action are not agitational in any meaningful sense. They are make-believe. The only people fooled are the socialists themselves, who mistrain their members to believe they are genuinely engaged in mass agitation. Similarly, small groups of socialists who declare themselves to be "activist groups" or parties are deluding themselves. Because of their small size, they remain propaganda groups, whatever they may think they are. But they are confused propaganda groups and therefore a lot less effective than they could be.

This does not mean that a propaganda group can't do things, that it just sits on the sideline lines when struggles erupt or focuses on discussing obscure theoretical issues. Socialist Alternative is not a discussion circle, we try to reach people beyond our ranks, involve them in political activity and win them to socialism. But our activity is determined by a clear recognition of what it is possible to achieve today and what our limitations are. We are primarily arguing our ideas – selling our paper, running information stalls, holding meetings, talking to individuals, organising study groups, selling books – not agitating for mass action or building rank and file opposition groups in the unions.

Nor does this approach mean that a propaganda group ignores the debates, the campaigns and struggles that are taking place in society all the time. Socialist Alternative tries to respond to all the major issues of the day, from attacks on workers' rights, the racist demonising of Muslims and refugees, gay bashing and anti-Aboriginal racism or the widening gulf between the super-rich and the rest of us and the threat of imperialist war.

Over the last 20 years Socialist Alternative has been active in dozens of different campaigns, including the campaigns against Pauline Hanson and the far right, the protests against government budget cuts, the refugee movement, the Marriage Equality campaign, the demonstrations against the Iraq and Afghanistan wars, the union mobilisations against WorkChoices, in support of Aboriginal rights, the anti-capitalist movement, support for Palestinian rights, the defence of the Maritime Union, Occupy and innumerable student protests. In a number of these campaigns and protests, such as the Marriage Equality campaign,[2] the Melbourne Campaign Against Racism and Fascism, the pro-Palestinian protests and the student campaign against education cuts, our members have played a leading or initiating role.

Our members are active as militants in their trade unions and in student unions. Socialist Alternative worker members have been involved in numerous strikes and union campaigns and at times, such as the fight for equal pay for women in the social and community services sector and strikes by warehouse workers, have played a prominent leading role.[3] We have done sustained strike support work in a whole series of other strikes from the 1998 Maritime Union dispute to the 2011 Baiada chicken factory strike.[4] Over the last decade we have been the largest left wing faction in the National Union of Students (NUS) and have been elected to various officer bearer positions. In NUS and the large number of local student unions where we are active we have fought to build a democratic, activist and politically engaged union that will stand up for students' rights.

While we can play an active role in small campaigns, individual strikes and in student politics, we recognise that we are in no position to initiate a broad fight back to challenge the bosses' neo-liberal agenda, rebuild the union movement or play a leading role in genuine mass movements like the ACTU's campaign against WorkChoices in 2005/2006 or the enormous protests against the war on Iraq in 2003. Instead we attempt to relate to people shaken up and radicalised by these movements and who are looking for political answers to explain why these attacks are happening and what can be done to change the world.

However we can't convince people to become active and useful socialists by preaching timeless truths about the nature of capitalism. We need to be able to confidently answer their concrete questions about the issues of the day and to refute the arguments of the right wing and the reformists. We participate in whatever movements that do arise to argue how they can win – for the need for mass action rather than relying on the ALP – and to explain how the drive to imperialist war and the attacks on workers' living standards are all the product of a capitalist system in which a wealthy minority lives off the labour of the mass of workers. In other words, we intervene to argue ideas – to make concrete propaganda – to try to win people radicalised by these protests to a socialist standpoint.

We also see intervening in these movements as vital training. It is a way to test our analysis and arguments about capitalism today. It is a way to hone the arguments of our existing members so that they can intervene more effectively and cohere a layer of people around us. It is a way to integrate new members recruited from these movements, as they have to go out and try to convince other people of our arguments about the road forward. It is a means to educate ourselves so that we can actually play a central leading role in the struggles and movements of the future, when we have accumulated more forces.

There is nothing unusual about Marxists being in a small minority in capitalist society. In fact, this has been the case for most of the century and a half since Marx and Engels founded the revolutionary socialist movement. There is a simple explanation for this fact: the ideas of this society are predominantly the ideas of the bosses. The owners of the means of production – the factories, the mines, the offices – also dominate the reproduction of ideas. The capitalists control the education system, the media, advertising, the courts, the government bureaucracy – all the institutions that mould ideas and values. But when the fabric of capitalist society is ruptured by revolt, socialist ideas can break the bosses' hold over the way workers think about their lives.

In other times, Marxists have to be prepared to be a minority, but not a passive minority. We form a nucleus that prepares for opportunities that unfold when radical outbursts occur. The classic example of this was the Emancipation of Labour Group, the first Russian Marxist group founded by Georgii Plekhanov in 1883, which I will examine in a subsequent chapter. It started as a tiny group in extremely unfavourable circumstances. Yet this isolated group eventually gave birth to a movement that shook the whole of Russian society in two great waves of revolution in 1905 and 1917, and led workers to power in October 1917.

Political clarification

The Emancipation of Labour Group planted the flag. They carved out a distinct Marxist tradition that paved the way for future generations of Russian Marxists. They provided a clear ideological critique of rival political currents. The first task of a small socialist group is ideological clarification, the sorting out of ideas, and the training of a group of dedicated revolutionaries in those ideas. Since groups like Socialist Alternative are primarily in the business of arguing ideas, we can only build on a secure foundation for the future if our ideas are as clear and precise as possible. The smaller the group, the greater the emphasis has to be on theory. Otherwise there is no way that it can survive. To borrow a metaphor from Leon Trotsky, a tiny axe can chop down the most gigantic tree, but only if the blade is sharp. Our ideas have to be finely honed.

But why is it so important to clarify our ideas now, when Marxism does not have a mass following? The answer is that an upsurge of revolt puts revolutionary politics to the most severe test. Any confusion, any major error can be disastrous for the whole working class movement.

We only have to look at the range of theoretical and strategic questions that Lenin and the Bolsheviks had to master in order to lead the Russian revolution to victory in 1917. They had to come to grips with the imperialist nature of World War I, the need for workers to turn the war into a civil war against their own ruling class. Lenin had to rediscover one of Marx's most important teachings: that the capitalist state had to be smashed for workers to come to power. In the period after the February revolution, Lenin had to break completely with his longstanding argument that a revolution that swept Tsarism aside would simply bring the bourgeoisie to power, that it would not flow over into a socialist revolution. And finally in order to lead the revolution to victory, Lenin needed to know when and how to launch an insurrection.

A large revolutionary party with strong working class roots, and with an established tradition and leadership and sizeable cadre, can survive for a period and continue to play a positive role in the class struggle even if some of its ideas are confused or just plain wrong.

However, a small organisation does not have anything like the same ballast. If it does not have a clear political understanding it is much more likely to go off the rails. At best it will stagnate and decay, at worst it will fragment. This is what happened to the Trotskyist movement in the 1940s and 1950s. There can be no doubt that the Trotskyists were the genuine revolutionaries of the time. But they inherited from Trotsky a wrong analysis of Russia and an overblown expectation of the prospects for revolutionary upheaval after the Second World War.

Trotsky rejected the idea that the Russian revolution had been totally defeated by a Stalinist counter-revolution that had brought to power a bureaucratic state capitalist ruling class that exploited the Russian working class. He argued that Russia was still a workers' state – albeit a degenerated one. He saw the Stalinist bureaucracy as an unstable layer balancing between the Russian working class and world imperialism. He predicted that the Stalinist regime would not survive the war. But instead of collapsing or being overthrown by workers, the Stalinist bureaucracy came out of the war as the second strongest power in the world and with half of Europe under its sway. New, supposedly Communist states were created in Eastern Europe without workers' revolutions taking place. How could the Trotskyists explain this development? Their confusion and disorientation shattered them into fragments. The majority made accommodations to Stalinism. Others dropped out in despair. Some refused to face up to reality and retreated into sectarian lunacy. Only a tiny minority, such as the founders of the International Socialist Tendency, came to terms with the fact that Russia was capitalist and imperialist.

Today, the need for clear, firm politics is just as great. Real opportunities exist internationally to rebuild the socialist movement. In country after country over the last two decades – from France to South Korea to Nigeria to numerous countries in Latin America to Greece to South Africa, to Spain, to more recently the US – we have seen concerted resistance to our rulers' free market, neo-liberal agenda. But that resistance has thrown up question after question that it is vital to resolve if the movement is to be rebuilt on a sound basis – what should be the socialist approach be to parties like Syriza in Greece or Podemos in Spain or to the emergence of Jeremy Corbyn in Britain, what stance do we take to the upsurge of Islamophobia and the revival of the far right, what sort of socialist organisation do we need?

The process of ideological clarification has taken different forms throughout the history of our movement. Different political problems had to be confronted at different times. For Marx and Engels the central task was establishing the core theoretical base of the revolutionary movement. That meant writing lengthy theoretical works. These were huge books like the three volumes of *Capital*, three more volumes of *Theories of Surplus Value* and the *Grundrisse*. These volumes were not written to be sold on protest marches. They were not propaganda works – many of them were not even published during Marx's lifetime. They were written to clarify Marx and Engels' own ideas, to develop a basic analysis of capitalist society. For the pioneers of revolutionary social-ism, it was necessary to establish the very foundations of the Marxist world-view, to discover and then to argue out in detail their theoretical conclusions. Of course, as I outline in a subsequent chapter, Marx and Engels did not devote all their energies to this path breaking theoretical work. They also played a central role in building revolution-ary organisations, actively intervening in the 1848 revolutions that swept Europe and writing numerous articles and popular pamphlets aimed at a working class readership.

Pioneering theoretical work on the scale of Marx's *Capital* is not the task of Socialist Alternative today. It is vital to develop Marxist theory to keep abreast of the compli-cated political and economic developments of world capitalism and new political and theoretical challenges are constantly being thrown up. However the core principles of Marxism are well established. We are standing on the shoulders of the giants of the revolutionary tradition who have gone before us. The path breaking theoretical work has already been done by Marx, Engels, Lenin, Trotsky, Luxemburg and many others. The task of Socialist Alternative today is a more modest one: to critically study and absorb their conclusions, to update them to deal with a constantly changing world system and to train a cadre that can fight for these ideas.

There is a sense though in which we are pioneers. The genuine revolutionary tradition of Marxism was buried by decades of Stalinist domination of the left and by well over a century of betrayals by the likes of the ALP. We have to re-establish the *real* Marxist tradition – that workers must emancipate themselves. The Stalinist system has collapsed but it has left a terrible legacy of confusion and cynicism about how fundamental social change can be achieved. This has been reinforced by the utter bankruptcy of social democratic parties, such as the ALP, which have repeatedly disillusioned their support-ers ,and the lack of a fighting stance by the reformist leaders of the union movement.

The challenge today in Australia and many other countries is to rebuild the social-ist movement largely from scratch and breathe life into the union movement and the broader left so that we can begin to turn the tide against our rulers. This is not simply an organisational task. Any revival of the left and the workers' movement will throw up a mass of new questions and confusions. Marxists will have to wage a vigorous ideological struggle if we are to take the movement forward on a sound basis.

In the 1930s the Trotskyists had to fight to keep alive the most basic idea of Marxism – the centrality of the working class in the struggle for socialism – which was being buried by the triumph of Stalinism in Russia and throughout the world Communist movement. In the 1950s Tony Cliff and a small band of revolutionaries in the Socialist Review Group in Britain had to fight to maintain the real Marxist tradition when sections of the Trotskyist movement itself started to capitulate to Stalinism. They had to help update Marxist theory to account for the post-war economic boom – an event that ran counter to the Trotskyists' predictions – and to explain the spread of Stalinism to Eastern Europe and China. Cliff and his collaborators helped develop an analysis known as the Permanent Arms Economy to explain the boom and the theory of state capitalism to explain the nature of Russia and China. But they never retreated completely to being simply a study circle. They began to delineate the tasks of a propaganda group as they produced and sold a regular publication.

One of the consistent themes in their discussions about what to do next was an insistence on a realistic assessment of the insignificant impact they could have in the short term, the need for patience and to carry out the basic work of establishing a core of Marxists capable of carrying the ideological arguments with individuals they met in movements such as the Campaign for Nuclear Disarmament. In this way they trained a cadre who, when the breaks came in the late sixties, could recruit significant numbers. Against enormous odds they came out of the political downturn of the long post war boom and grew significantly during the upturn of the sixties and seventies.

Building cadre is key

If the first task of a propaganda group is ideological clarification – establishing a rock solid commitment to the theory and traditions of Marxism – then the second is to build a bigger group. Socialist Alternative does not presume it is the sole nucleus around which a future mass party will be cohered. There is no straight forward road to the construction of such a party. Other political currents will almost certainly emerge out of the struggles of the future that will be an important part of that process.

The successful unity in 2013 between Socialist Alternative and the Revolutionary Socialist Party (RSP), which came from a different political tradition, reflects in a small way the possibilities that can open up in the future for genuine revolutionary regroupment.[5] We can't, however, passively sit and wait for other revolutionary forces to emerge. We need to actively build and recruit today to begin to lay the basis for a mass revolutionary party that can lead future workers' struggles to victory.

Recruitment is vital but by itself it is useless if the people recruited aren't educated in Marxism, if they aren't trained in revolutionary activity, and if they aren't politically integrated into the organisation. What's more, to build from a small revolutionary group into a mass party is no simple linear process, whereby the group grows by 20 per cent each year until it has tens of thousands of members. There are periods of great political advance and there are others of retreat. In the periods of advance a socialist organisation can grow extremely rapidly, indeed such growth is vital if we are to build a mass party. But if we do draw in large numbers of new people, what guarantee is there that Socialist Alternative will remain a cohered, disciplined and principled revolutionary organisation? How do we educate new fighters in Marxist theory? Won't we be swamped?

Lenin had to face exactly this problem during the 1905 revolution in Russia. The revolutionary upsurge saw tens of thousands of workers move towards the small Bolshevik nucleus. Lenin not only argued that it was vital to draw in these new people; he counted on the "solid core of social democrats" – the party's *cadre* – to influence, educate and train the new recruits. And he relied on the strength and training of this cadre to prevent the party's politics and traditions being overwhelmed and forgotten.

> We Bolsheviks...have demanded class consciousness from those joining the party, we have insisted on the tremendous importance of continuity in the party's development, we have preached discipline and demanded that every party member be trained in one or other of the party organisations.[6]

This cadre, this "solid core", is just as important in times of retreat, when workers suffer setbacks. In order to hold a revolutionary organisation together in times of defeat theory is even more paramount. When the going is tough a much higher level of theoretical agreement is necessary to hold a propaganda group together because a small group without roots in the working class is inherently more unstable than a mass party. You can't survive on the basis of a few slogans and catchphrases; you need a more sophisticated analysis. The cadre has to be steeled. That means a high degree of political demarcation from those on the left who don't agree with key aspects of Marxism. There can be no compromises, no concessions to soft left ideas that fudge key political questions. However a larger organisation in periods when the struggle is surging forward can be more open. It can link up with other radicalising currents and recruit on the basis of agreement on a few central slogans.

Today socialists are operating in a frustrating and complicated political period. There is little support for the neo-liberal economic agenda that is being constantly rammed down our throats; little support for the US's imperialist adventures. Internationally we have seen an increasing political polarisation. The savage austerity measures imposed in the wake of the 2007/2008 world financial crisis have led on the one hand to the rise of far right parties like Marine Le Pen's National Front in France, the entry of open Nazis into the German parliament and the victory of Donald Trump in the US and on the other hand to a surge of support for left wing British Labour Party leader Jeremy Corbyn and of Bernie Sanders in the US, the rise of Podemos in Spain and in Greece the election victory (and subsequent terrible betrayal) by the left wing Syriza party. World politics are being transformed. Australia has not, as yet, been as devastatingly impacted by the drawn out world economic crisis. Nonetheless working class living standards are under considerable pressure and the divide between the fabulous wealth of the tiny group of billionaires at the top of society and the mass of people relentlessly increases.

When serious forces, such as the trade union leaders, give workers and students a chance to demonstrate their discontent – at the union rallies against WorkChoices in 2005/2006 and the campaign around the Marriage Equality plebiscite in 2017 – they do so in unparalleled numbers. Yet there is no concerted ongoing opposition. Neither the union leaders, nor the ALP, nor the Greens are prepared to unleash a challenge to the ruling class's agenda. This leads to pessimism about the possibility of real change. If you don't have a clear analysis of the political situation, you can succumb to impressionistic moods and miss out on the opportunities to build a revolutionary organisation that currently exist and will open up in the future. But growth won't happen automatically. It is never plain sailing. We can't predict the exact contours of future struggles and radicalisations. What we can do is to attempt to train a cadre that is clear on the nature of the political period and is able to respond to make the most of the opportunities that do open up.

So building a socialist organisation involves more than just recruiting new people, it also involves developing them into revolutionary cadre. What does this mean? The newer members, comrades who have only been in the group a year or two, have to be trained in the basics of Marxism. But Marxism doesn't just reside in books. For those ideas to become a material force they have to be embodied in individuals, they have to take an organisational form. If the organisation is to survive and grow, its members have to be able to argue socialist ideas to uncommitted people, to convince them that they should become active revolutionaries. Political education serves little purpose if it is separated from building a socialist organisation. There is no point being an expert on the Marxist theory of imperialism if you do nothing to build a revolutionary organisation today. Indeed one of the best tests of whether a comrade understands a particular area of Marxist politics is having to argue that position with people outside the organisation.

But there is more to being a cadre than understanding Marxist politics and being able to argue for those ideas. Cadre must be able to scientifically evaluate the development of the class struggle and society generally, in order to work out how to take advantage of these developments. They must understand and be able to carry out the mechanics of building the organisation. They must understand the tactics: the various twists and turns that a socialist organisation has to go through to begin to lay the basis for a mass party. They must be able to relate to other forces and lead workers and students outside the ranks of the organisation in struggle. Such a cadre is not trained overnight. Nor are they trained without hard work, without an intense effort in theoretical education and in the practical tasks of building a socialist organisation. But without the development and continual expansion of that layer of cadre, a revolutionary organisation builds on sand.

Identifying your audience

The next question that arises for a propaganda group is: at whom should it aim its ideas? What is its audience? It can't for the present win the masses, but who can it win? Unless a socialist organisation can answer this question, then it is yet again on the road to oblivion. It is not enough to have formally correct but abstract ideas – to understand everything in Marx's *Capital*. Marxists must understand how to concretely apply those ideas. They have to be able to answer the central political question: what do we do next?

Identifying an audience, creating a periphery around your organisation for Marxist politics, is not an easy task. An audience is not a static body of people. It changes depending on political circumstances, the depth of the crisis in society, the ebbs and flows of the class struggle and the size of the socialist group. As well, it is not just a question of saying that at this particular moment, this specific group of people are our audience. You then have to be able to concretely work out how to relate to them, to find the issues that will give you an "in", to patiently and consistently debate the questions that have a cutting edge with these people.

Traditionally Marxists had a certain guide as to their audience: they tried to relate to the vanguard – the most politically conscious section of the working class and the already established left-wing forces. So when Marx and Engels published their most important propaganda work, *The Communist Manifesto*, they were not aiming it at the mass of workers, but at those who already considered themselves communists. Marx and Engels polemicised against the erroneous conceptions of these early socialists – their conspiratorial methods, their utopianism, their elitism – and tried to win a minority to their world view.

Similarly, after the 1917 Bolshevik revolution, when Lenin established a new Communist International (the Comintern), he won his first supporters from the existing socialist movement. The small bands of supporters of the Russian revolution aimed their fire at the reformist parties of the Second Socialist International – the parties that had betrayed the working class by their support for their own ruling classes in World War I. The Bolsheviks hoped to win over cadres from the left wing of these reformist parties. Only when they had regrouped these forces could they appeal to the broader unorganised masses.

Again, when the Trotskyists were expelled from the Stalinised Communist parties in the late 1920s, they did not immediately turn their backs on the CPs. The CPs still, by and large, had the support of many of the most class-conscious workers. The small Trotskyist groups had to win over some of the better elements in or influenced by the CPs. They had to pound away arguing about what was wrong with Comintern policies.

That was how they recruited their initial cadre. To attempt to jump over this stage, to appeal directly to people not involved in socialist politics, would have led nowhere. For the reality is that when such people begin to move politically, they look for leadership to the already existing vanguard.

Marxists had to implant themselves in that vanguard if they hoped to lead the masses in the future. Those revolutionaries in the early 1930s who tried to force the pace artificially, to jump over the necessary stage of political development, came to grief. Some of them ignored or dismissed the Communist parties and their entire membership. They said you had to build among workers who had not been infected by the virus of Stalinism. They were quickly demoralised and collapsed. Others, declaring that it was a sectarian and conservative course just to win over individuals or groups of people from the CPs and hence train a cadre, argued for mass work to build a new party. They too got nowhere and began to retreat from Marxist principles in the direction of opportunism as they chased an illusory audience for their mass work.

However, this traditional approach for building a Marxist organisation presents today's revolutionaries with a serious problem. There has been no organised political vanguard in any meaningful sense in Australia or in most other advanced capitalist countries since the 1970s. There is no mass organisation of radicals of any description in Australia, nor any significant current of politicised workers that revolutionaries can orient to. There are, of course, in many workplaces a few workers who are active in the union or more left wing than most workers. But they do not form an organised layer that revolutionaries can relate to on an ongoing basis.

Nor are there ongoing campaigns that we can relate to that are radicalising and organising into activity significant bodies of people. There have been a significant number of mass protests over the last two decades, such as the Marriage Equality rallies, the union rallies against WorkChoices, the enormous demonstrations against the Iraq war, the demonstrations against Pauline Hanson first time round and the 1998 Maritime Union dispute. They did not, however, lead to the emergence of ongoing organised movements that provided a significant audience for socialists. The most important – but short-lived – exception to this pattern was the anti-capitalist movement that developed amongst a layer of young people in the wake of the Seattle protest against the World Trade Organisation in 1999 and the blockade of the World Economic Forum at Melbourne's Crown Casino in 2000. For about 18 months the anti-capitalist movement provided Marxists with a concentrated audience of people looking for an alternative to capitalism. It opened up the possibility of quite rapid growth.

When such movements do develop it is vital for socialists to quickly seize the opportunity and to throw themselves into them. When there is a layer of people being radicalised around a particular issue, revolutionaries have to relate in a *practical* way to that issue or struggle. While small socialist organisations will rarely be in a position to lead major struggles, when these struggles do occur, socialists can't just stand on the sidelines preaching the general ideas of socialism. They have to be able to relate their general socialist ideas to the specific issue. Socialists have to be able to argue a strategy for winning the struggle, to put forward concrete proposals that point the way forward. They have to draw out the lessons at all stages of the struggle, to point out the role of the police, the media, parliament, the ALP, the trade union officials and so on.

Most importantly, socialists must be able to link the particular issue, whether it is attacks on workers' rights, racist attacks or cuts to education, to broader questions such as the capitalists' neo-liberal agenda, the nature of imperialism, the role of the working class and how we can change society. But let's be clear, most of the time intervention by a small socialist organisation means intervening in political debates that occur either in society as a whole, or among the milieu in which they are working. Whether or not the group is involved in a specific campaign or struggle, the discussions the group needs to have with other activists, if they are to influence them in a socialist direction, have to go a long way beyond just campaign tactics and strategy.

The fact that there is no organised working class vanguard or cohered body of radical activists or movements that attract ongoing, large-scale support does not mean that there is no audience of people open to socialist arguments. The relentless ruling class offensive against workers, the never-ending "war on terror", the continual attacks on democratic rights and the failure of the ALP and union leaders to offer any concerted resistance continually throw up an audience of people looking for an alternative to the horrors of capitalism. But by and large these are scattered individuals who are relatively new to political activism and have little knowledge of Marxist ideas.

Relating to students – a milieu to work in

The long term aim of a small revolutionary organisation is to get bigger – and primarily, to have an influence in the working class. Yet the leap between the present and the future is a continuing source of debate among socialists. It seems common sense that, if we understand that only the working class can lead a socialist revolution, then we should build among workers. So why does Socialist Alternative put considerable effort into building among students, and what has that to do with the leap from the isolation of a small group to the influence of a mass workers' party?

The experience of working class militants in surviving in the workplace – and the need to involve a majority of the workforce in any successful industrial activity – makes them much more practical than students. If they have been involved in any political activity as workers, it will likely have been through their union, an organisation of some size and strength, which has the potential to deliver action. A small revolutionary organisation simply can't do that and as a consequence will not seem a serious force in comparison to a union. But because often a small minority among students *can* carry out meaningful activity – hold a lively protest or occupation initiate a campaign or win office in the student union – quite small groups of socialists can realistically play a leading role and be taken more seriously on the campuses.

For one thing, they can organise groups of students to do much more than is possible in a similar situation at work. Just think of the regular information stalls, lecture announcements, poster runs and club meetings socialists can hold on campus and the small protests and speak outs they can help organise and the election campaigns they can participate in. For these reasons a socialist intervention can have more impact. But as well socialists can more easily find on campus an audience that can be won over on the basis of an intellectual argument, rather than on the basis of what they can deliver. That is why for any socialist group a milieu of student activists is one of the best places to gain the vital experience they need and help to orient the group away from sectarian abstention.

Moreover students can play a role in social upheaval, and they can genuinely fight for their rights. Their volatility can mean that after long periods of calm, they may be the first to burst into rebellion. In the sixties they took the lead in country after country, drawing workers in behind them.[7] They have played a similar role in more recent years in countries such as France and Chile. Student struggles are not some Mickey Mouse affair for revolutionaries to "practise" on. Socialists can gain invaluable experience and train a cadre capable of leading important struggles on the campuses.

So Socialist Alternative doesn't relate to students because students are somehow more worthy or more left wing than workers. We certainly don't think they can lead a future revolution – but they can play an important part in social upheaval. Students' struggles and concerns are legitimate and can play a role in radicalising many students in the here and now. Because of their youth, generally different lifestyle and class position from workers, especially older workers who have suffered years of defeat and have family responsibilities, perhaps a mortgage and/or a career, students are more likely to take seriously a small group of socialists with not much more than their ideas to offer.

The argument for relating to students does not in any way imply that *most* students are likely to be interested in left-wing politics nor that the campuses are currently hot beds of protest. Unfortunately we have gone through a prolonged period of political retreat on campus.

It is certainly not the case that because students are more "educated" they are likely to be more radical. Actually, the main aim of education is to train people to work for industry and to carry out technical tasks, and so for the most part, students will be taught, and will accept, some variant of the dominant ideology of capitalism. However, there is an inbuilt contradiction in the bosses' need for education. If you want creative workers, you have to allow a certain amount of debate and critical thought. During those few years of tertiary study, students have the possibility of dealing in ideas in a way that most other groups in society do not. The rhetoric of academic freedom and exploration clashes with the reality of an increasingly corporatised education system. The gap between how the world *is*, and how it *ought* to be means that a minority of students will be interested in discussing and questioning ideas.

The nature of student life provides opportunities for small groups of revolutionaries. If a socialist group is to be able to learn to make arguments that are not purely abstract, it needs a "milieu" in which to work, where its members have to answer people's arguments, convince others to get involved in activity, of the best way to win a campaign and so on. Socialists have to learn to lead, i.e. how to convince others of ideas they initially don't totally agree with.

All small socialist groups can have tendencies to abstract propagandism. This pulls them away from relating to peoples' real concerns. But consciously looking for ways to interact with others we may be able to influence on an ongoing basis is one way to minimise this danger. The important phrase here is *others we may be able to influence*. An individual socialist in a workplace – up against a union bureaucracy that can produce thousands of leaflets, get on the evening news, demand that other unions do this or that – will have a hard time convincing her fellow workers that a socialist group of a few hundred or a few thousand, even if they were all trade unionists, knows how to better run a strike. This is definitely not an argument against socialists attempting to lead at work. Even if they can only recruit the occasional individual, steady union work and leading the occasional industrial action adds to the general knowledge and experience of the organisation. It helps build a layer of members who have some feel for how to make arguments relevant in unions. It is simply that union activism cannot be the central focus for building a small socialist group.

Students relating to workers

Won't a group with a large number of student or ex-student members be incapable of relating to workers when it's needed? It's true that such a group can develop ways of doing things which might seem strange to some blue-collar workers. However, this is much less the case than in the past. Before the massive expansion of tertiary education in the post World War II boom, students were elite, with a completely different background, lifestyle and expectations from workers. In Australia many of them supported reactionary movements, for example acting as strikebreakers in the 1917 mass strike and backing fascism in the 1930s. However, even then, for all the reasons above, a minority were pulled towards socialism. And those small numbers could provide an important nucleus for socialist organisations which were to lead masses of workers. The Bolsheviks in Russia had many students who were recruited to Marxism. Just think of the background of leading figures such as Lenin, Trotsky, Krupskaya and others, and people like Rosa Luxemburg in Germany or Antonio Gramsci in Italy. They had all become socialists while students.

When workers are involved in mass struggle, they can become open to new ideas on a rapidly expanding scale. Workers can take revolutionary ideas more seriously than previously simply because they realise they need new ideas to win their struggles. But very importantly, it depends on whether there is a serious organisation on offer. With even some hundreds of students in a single city, let alone thousands, an organisation could intervene effectively to offer strike support and ideological argument. The very process of this kind of work would develop and change the existing members, who would have to learn to be sensitive to workers' needs, ideas and experiences in order to intervene. Some of this can be learned before an upswing in struggle, but it cannot be seriously tested in the absence of serious mass, radical struggles.

The importance of a propaganda routine

Because there currently is no single issue that is radicalising large numbers of people, socialists have to be able to relate to people on a range of questions. We have to be able to take up the specific issues that they are concerned about and explain how they fit into a Marxist analysis of what's wrong with the world. We have to be able to talk to them about everything from the growing gap between rich and poor, the "war on terror" or anti-Aboriginal racism to more general questions like why the working class can change society, why Russia wasn't socialist and the way forward for socialists today. To intersect with all these scattered individuals, revolutionaries need a high profile.

That's why we in Socialist Alternative put great emphasis on doing regular information stalls, where we sell our paper *Red Flag*, in city streets and on university campuses. We make a concerted mobilisation for virtually all demonstrations, whether large or small. On the demonstrations we have information stalls, sell *Red Flag* and march as a contingent – a Red Bloc – made up of our members and supporters. At the end of the demonstration we usually have a well-advertised meeting aimed at those on the march who are interested in finding out more about socialist ideas or to debate out whatever controversial issues have arisen in the campaign. All our major branches hold well-advertised public meetings, and our clubs on campuses hold regular forums. Over the last decade we have established our annual Marxism Conference over the Easter weekend in Melbourne as the largest left wing conference in Australia and our large Socialism Conference in Sydney has now also become a regular event.

We have established a regular propaganda routine that helps us to intersect with the scattered individuals interested in left wing ideas and ensures that we actually follow them up, talk to them personally to try to convince them to get active as a socialist, and invite them to our regular Marxist Discussion Groups, public meetings and other events and demonstrations. A stable propaganda routine of regular paper sales, discussion groups and branch meetings, campus work and following up people we meet, forces us to look outwards, to address people beyond our ranks, people who only agree with some of our arguments. It helps prevent the organisation from becoming inward-looking. It keeps the group active, and provides a discipline that can help ward off passivity.

Of course, a propaganda routine is no guarantee against complacency. Routine can easily become routinism. That is why revolutionaries must be ready to break and adapt their established routine to meet changed conditions, to make new interventions. Our audience can change quickly as the political climate shifts. Socialists won't always be appealing to scattered individuals. Flexibility is key. But without a stable propaganda routine, without regular branch meetings and sales of a publication, without the systematic following up of potential supporters, a socialist organisation will be in no position to take advantage of opportunities that do open up.

For well over two decades, workers' living standards and trade union rights have been under relentless attack, under both Liberal and Labor governments, and there is no sign of the bosses' offensive letting up. When you add to this the ever-looming environmental crisis, the prospect of decade after decade of brutal imperialist war, rampant Islamophobia and ongoing attacks on democratic rights you can understand why there is growing unease among millions of workers and students. Yet while year after year social inequality gets worse and worse the rich and powerful seem never satiated. And still we are told we are living through boom years here in Australia.

We cannot predict how and when these growing tensions will come to a head. However, we can be confident that at some point there will be a major revival in working class struggle. The decisive struggles of the future will pose both major opportunities and difficulties for socialists. The unfolding of the struggle will be complicated and tortuous. Nothing will be straightforward. To make the most of these challenges, we have to prepare today by deepening our political understanding, by testing ourselves, by confronting the tasks of the moment. One of the most important tasks of the moment is to grow. To the extent that socialists can grow now, when furious struggles are not raging, we will be better placed to intervene and offer an alternative when workers and students are on the move. And it is important to emphasise that there *are* opportunities to grow today, not just when there are sizeable protests in the streets but in the quieter patches in between.

It is also important to be clear that the growth of a socialist group is only in part determined by the external political environment. Short of a mass radicalisation or a sharp radicalisation amongst a minority of young people such as the anti-capitalist movement of the early 2000s, socialists will not recruit hand over fist, but a propaganda group can make headway against the pace of events. All sorts of internal factors – the coherence of the group, the clarity of the group's perspectives and the experience and confidence of the members – can be even more important in recruiting the next ten people as the ebbs and flows of the class struggle.

To summarise

So let's summarise the central tasks of a propaganda group. The first is political clarity: only by deepening their political understanding can Marxists lay a sound foundation for the future. Second, a propaganda group has to aim to grow in size and at the same time develop a layer of members – a cadre – that understands Marxist ideas and is able to apply those ideas in the specific circumstances of today. Putting those ideas into practice means identifying an audience for Marxism, establishing how to relate to that audience, and finally doing the detailed work – organising and carrying out routine propaganda work and not-so-routine interventions in the debates and struggles that break out – that is necessary to recruit new forces.

Finally socialists cannot jump over the necessary stages of the development they have to go through. In the present situation in Australia, and given the length and qualitative experience of the majority of our members, Socialist Alternative cannot be anything like the Bolsheviks in 1917 or the Communist Party in the 1930s. They had been through decades of major political and social crises, not a long drawn out period of a low level of struggle. Those decades of mass struggle challenged them in a way that socialists in Australia today have not yet experienced. A revolutionary organisation is steeled in significant ideological debates and major struggles. We cannot conjure these up.

CHAPTER TWO

Karl Marx and Frederick Engels: revolutionary activists and party builders

In 1845, right at the start of his revolutionary career, Karl Marx wrote in his *Theses on Feuerbach* "philosophers have only *interpreted* the world...the point, however, is to *change* it."[8] This statement represented Marx's settling of his account with his academic training in philosophy. All his subsequent research and writings were aimed at laying the basis for a movement that could overthrow capitalism. In this sense they were all practical works. They aimed either to clarify his own ideas so that he could intervene more effectively in the struggle or were writings that directly armed workers to fight for their self-emancipation and helped construct a revolutionary party to lead that struggle.

Yet if you pick up virtually any academic work on Marx, he is presented as a middle-class intellectual, cut off from the workers' movement, who sat in the British Museum concocting obscure philosophical theories. Terrell Carver in the *Cambridge Companion to Marx* wrote that he "left political organisation almost entirely to others...nor was he... ever involved directly in the politics of his land of exile" and "was not himself a direct actor in German politics."[9] The reality is the exact opposite. Marx and Engels devoted their entire adult lives to practical intervention in the workers' movement and to building revolutionary organisation. As Engels said at Marx's graveside in 1883:

> Marx was before all else a revolutionist...fighting was his element. And he fought with a passion, a tenacity and a success such as few could rival.[10]

There are two main sources of the myth of Marx "the great thinker". Firstly there are the pretensions of academics – their elitism and self-importance. Academics massively overvalue academic learning. For them it is ideas that change the world – not the struggle of the untutored masses. Marx and Engels totally rejected this elitist approach: "Ideas

27

cannot carry out anything at all. In order to carry out ideas men are needed who can exert practical force."[11] The second source of the myth is reformist writers who want to draw a sharp line between Marx – the well-meaning thinker – and Lenin – the hard headed party builder, whereas in fact Marx prepared the ground for Lenin.

By 1845 Marx and Engels as communists saw their task as linking up with other fighters, particularly among the working class – the only class that had the interest and the capacity to end class rule. Their strategy in the mid-1840s was to differentiate themselves from other currents that competed for a working class audience by critiquing their views. They joined the Communist Correspondence Committees to debate with other communist currents scattered across Europe and via them find a working class audience.

Marx and Engels are usually presented as intellectuals who dominated the workers – but the reality was quite the opposite. They had to prove themselves to communist workers by practical activity. Up to the 1840s most working class communists were organised in secret societies which conspired to "make" the revolution. Revolution was seen as an armed coup which would enable the communists to establish an "educational dictatorship" that would eventually usher in a classless society. By the mid-1840s some communist workers were beginning to break with this elitist view and were looking to mobilise the masses. It was one such group of exiled German revolutionary workers – the League of the Just – that Marx and Engels linked up with. Initially they had a standoff-ish approach to Marx and Engels, as they did not trust intellectuals. But after a period of collaboration Marx and Engels were asked to write a program for the organisation, which was renamed the Communist League.

The program was *The Communist Manifesto*. Marx and Engels saw writing this program as a central task for educating effective fighters. It would provide a perspective, a line of march. Marx and Engels were not abstract theorists but nor were they mindless activists. They had a scientific approach to revolutionary politics that emphasised study, research and clarification of their ideas.

The Communist Manifesto reflected the birth of a new political current that broke decisively with the old elitist conspiratorial approach and based itself on working-class self-emancipation.[12] It was a guiding light for Communist intervention in the wave of revolt that was about to sweep Europe. It was published just in time, in February 1848. Starting with a workers' revolt in Paris, over the next 18 months there were 50 armed uprisings.

Marx and Engels played a prominent role, first in Belgium where Marx headed the Communist League and used money from an inheritance to buy arms for the workers. Then, after Marx's expulsion from Belgium, Marx and Engels and 300-400 exiled members of the Communist League returned to Germany. Marx established a base in Cologne, in the most industrial part of Germany. He and his supporters published a daily paper, which with a readership of 6,000 became one of the most influential revolutionary papers. Marx and Engels played a leading role in the Cologne Democratic Society, and other Communist League members headed the 8,000-strong Workers' Association.

But the revolution went down to defeat, betrayed by wavering middle-class democrats who would not mobilise to overthrow the old order because they feared the workers. Marx retreated to London to reorganise the Communist League. Engels went to Baden to fight in the final military campaign of the revolution. But before doing so, in a final defiant gesture, they printed the last issue of their paper entirely in red ink.

To recohere the Communist League, in March 1850 Marx and Engels published *the Address of the Central Committee to the Communist League*. It summed up the lessons of the revolution and included some blunt self-criticisms. The key point was that workers could place no reliance on the middle class. They concluded – as against the more limited demands of middle class forces who "want to bring the revolution to an end as quickly as possible...it is...our task to make the revolution permanent"[13] – that is, to carry it forward to a socialist revolution. The address was written in the hope that the revolution would revive, but by mid-1850 no revival was in sight. So Marx and Engels set their task as preparing for the next upsurge, publishing key works like *Revolution and Counter-revolution in Germany*.

There followed a prolonged lull in the class struggle from 1851-1864. The Communist League was wound up following a split, and Marx and Engels concentrated on research. This is the period that is used as evidence of Marx's abandonment of active party politics. But it is not true. The prime focus of Marx's "swotting", as he termed it, was to strengthen the Communist forces – "the Marx party". Throughout this period Marx and Engels maintained a nucleus of experienced comrades so they would be able to take advantage of any revival of the movement. This is why "the Marx party" was able to quickly win the leadership of the next phase of struggle. They had clarified a program around which they cohered a group of supporters.

Throughout the lean years Marx and Engels intervened where they could in the movement. By 1863 there were signs of revival – the significant support in the British working class for the anti-slavery cause in the US Civil War, a peasant revolt in Poland and working class revival in Germany. This led in September 1864 to the establishment by British trade union leaders, in alliance with radicals on the continent, of the International Working Men's Association.

Marx was involved from the start and within a month had effectively assumed the leadership.[14] Marx and his fellow Communist Eccarius played a key role in drafting the rules and founding documents of the International. This meant that despite the diverse coalition involved, the International was founded on a principled basis. Its famous declaration proclaimed: "The emancipation of the working classes must be conquered by the working classes themselves."[15]

Marx was involved not just in writing key documents but in all the practical details, including finances and issuing membership cards. The International grew rapidly from its interventions in a series of strikes – the 1866 tailors' strike in London and Edinburgh, the 1867 Paris bronze-workers' strike, the 1868 Geneva building trade strike and the bloody Belgian miners' revolt of 1868. Marx helped co-ordinate the strike support work. By 1869, when membership peaked, it was the largest international workers' organisation yet. Inside the International Marx fought for women's involvement in the face of strident opposition from the anarchists. The Marxists campaigned for equal pay and supported the election of a prominent woman activist, Harriet Law, to the leadership. Marx and Engels also championed support for national liberation struggles, in particular the Irish revolt against British rule, again in the face of anarchist opposition.

In 1871 the International faced its major test – the Paris Commune, when workers rose up and seized control of Paris for three months. Members of the International were prominent in the leadership but unfortunately hardly any of them were Marxists with a clear idea of how to take the revolution forward. Lack of decisive leadership contributed to the Commune's defeat. Marx did all he could to aid the revolt– sending leading Marxists to Paris, including the Russian socialist Elisaveta Tomanovskaya, who played a prominent role in organising the Women's Union for the Defence of Paris. Marx's most important intervention was his booklet *The Civil War in France,* which quickly became his most widely-read work. Marx became very well known as the ruling classes of all Europe launched a frenzied attack on the Commune, branding Marx as the evil instigator of the revolt.

The International went into decline after the Commune, and there was a decisive split with the anarchists. But the Marxists continued to build. In Germany the first mass workers' party was formed. Marx and Engels were heavily involved with the German party – making a series of major interventions, including writing *The Critique of the Gotha Program* in opposition to reformist trends in the party. After Marx's death in 1883 Engels continued his work of building the rapidly growing international socialist movement. Engels' reading reflected his key role: he read three German, two English, one Italian and one Austrian daily socialist papers, plus two German, seven Austrian, one French, three American, two Italian, one Polish, one Bulgarian, one Spanish and one Bohemian weeklies.[16]

To sum up

Practical activity – intervention in mass struggles and debates and even in much smaller struggles and arguments – is vitally important for Marxists, because unlike virtually every other political current on the left we recognise that an enlightened minority of educated people cannot change the world; the masses must do it themselves. Furthermore, it is only in the course of struggle that the masses can educate themselves to run society.

So the task of Marxists is not to "educate" the working class so that they understand that they are exploited and oppressed by capitalism. Their own life experience and struggles teaches them that there are bosses and workers with counterposed interests. Nor is it the task of Marxists to teach the working class how to fight back. Over the last two hundred years workers all over the world have been amazingly inventive in their struggles. They did not need Marxists to come up with the idea of trade unions, picket lines, strikes, sit-downs, factory occupations, shop stewards, strike committees, workers' militias, boycotts, solidarity actions, black bans, workers' councils and soviets.

Nevertheless clear ideas are vital. When the masses move, we need a revolutionary organisation that can argue a way forward. But where do "correct ideas" come from? They come in large part from the practical experience of the masses in struggle. Communist theory is a summing up of the historical experience of the class struggle and the development of capitalist society. The role of Marxist leadership is to apply the lessons of the past experience of the working class movement to the debates and battles of today; so that every time workers move into battle, they don't have to reinvent the wheel. It is in the course of attempting to argue a way forward for the working class movement that revolutionaries learn how to lead, learn how to apply their theoretical ideas to the tasks of the moment, learn tactics and strategy.

This is precisely how Marx developed his own ideas. He learned from the revolutions of 1848 that workers could have no trust in any section of the capitalist class or the petty bourgeois democrats. They had to rely on their own strength and organisation. The Paris Commune was decisive for Marx's theoretical development. The Commune showed how workers could take over and run society. It also showed there was no point trying to reform the existing state. It had to be smashed and a new workers' state developed. There is no way Marx could have developed these central concepts by just sitting reading books on philosophy in the British Museum. It was detailed study of the history of the workers' movement combined with his key role in *leading* the workers' movement that enabled him to make these theoretical breakthroughs.

CHAPTER THREE

Plekhanov and the foundation of Marxism in Russia

G eorgii Plekhanov was the path breaker who played a central role in founding the Marxist movement in Russia in the 1880s. He helped forge a new revolutionary tradition that broke from the populism (which looked to "the people" as an undifferentiated mass) that had long dominated radical politics in Russia and instead looked to the working class as *the* force to transform society. Plekhanov helped prepare the way for Lenin and Trotsky and the successful workers' revolution of October 1917.

Plekhanov joined the radical movement in 1875 as a 19 year old engineering student. Thousands of students were being drawn into revolutionary activity against the oppressive Tsarist dictatorship. Russia was an overwhelmingly rural society but old feudal Russia was undergoing dramatic changes under the impact of capitalist development. Radical students and intellectuals believed that they could play a decisive role in hurrying up the pace of change. They believed that poor, backward Russia could skip over the stage of capitalist industrial development and establish a society based on the existing peasant villages – the rural communes – which radical students idealised as egalitarian and the basis of a future socialist society.

At the start of the 1870s a wave of student revolutionaries strongly influenced by anarchism went to the countryside to rouse the peasantry to revolt. Their slogan was – "to the people". Hence they were called populists – Narodniks in Russian. But the peasants were not in a rebellious mood in the 1870s and tended to see the middle class students as alien intruders. Isolated from mass support, the young revolutionaries became easy targets for Tsarist oppression.[7] In 1874 alone 4000 were imprisoned.

The response of many populists to this setback was: if the peasants were not yet ready to act, the revolutionaries had to act on their own. In line with their anarchist politics they formed a tight knit conspiratorial organisation, Land and Liberty, and began to resort to terrorism. On 24 January 1878 a woman student, Vera Zasulich, shot at the chief of the St Petersburg police, who had sentenced a political prisoner to a brutal flogging. There was widespread sympathy for her action. Indeed, a jury acquitted her! A series of assassination attempts soon followed.

Plekhanov, who had established a reputation as a dynamic organiser, quickly became a leader of Land and Liberty. Most famous was his leading role in an illegal demonstration in Kazan Square in December 1876. Hundreds of students and young workers had gathered to protest against the Tsarist authorities. A young man delivered an impassioned address. The crowd shouted in response: "Hail to the socialist revolution! Hail to Land and Liberty!"[18] Hardly had the first words of the speech been pronounced when the shrill whistles of the police sounded. Before the speech was over the police had started to arrest people. A melee ensued and Plekhanov escaped. But he had put himself irrevocably outside the law – for he had been the orator.

Plekhanov carried brass knuckles, practised the use of the dagger and slept with a revolver under his pillow. More significantly for his subsequent political development, he did something entirely new: he began to carry out agitation amongst factory workers. In the 1870s workers formed only a minute proportion of the Russian population, but they were becoming increasingly militant. In March 1878 and again in January 1879, Plekhanov was heavily involved in strikes by textile workers who sought the assistance of the revolutionary students. Plekhanov organised a strike fund, drew up leaflets on behalf of the workers and organised their distribution at other factories. Yet it was not simply that workers were militant. They also proved much more open to revolutionary ideas than the peasants. The radical students established organised groups of worker activists who adhered to socialist ideas and built up a genuine base in working class suburbs.

In 1879 Land and Liberty polarised between those who emphasised mass agitation and those who focused on terrorism. Plekhanov led the opposition to the emphasis on terrorism. Plekhanov was not yet a Marxist. He believed there was a role for terrorism but that it should not be the *main* activity. Although Plekhanov had organised successfully amongst workers, he still argued for an emphasis on agitation amongst the peasantry. At this stage he tended to view workers as just a section of the peasantry, albeit the "most enlightened representatives of the peasantry."[19]

The debate came to a head over the issue of assassinating the Tsar. In April 1879 a failed attempt to shoot the Tsar led to a wave of repression. The terrorist faction – a clear majority – formed a new organisation, Narodnaya Volya (The People's Will). Plekhanov was isolated. Most people in radical circles sympathised with the terrorists who for a few years had an impressive organisation. Indeed in March 1881 they succeeded in assassinating the Tsar. In contrast Plekhanov's new organisation, The General Redivision (not exactly the most scintillating name), never really got off the ground. By January 1880 wide scale arrests had forced Plekhanov to escape abroad.

In exile in Geneva, Switzerland, Plekhanov began a program of rigorous theoretical study, in particular of the writings of Marx and Engels. The fundamental idea of the populists was peasant socialism based on the rural communes which were collectively owned by the village population. The populists argued that there was no need for a capitalist stage of development in Russia to build up industry and lay the basis for an advanced socialist society. Plekhanov began an intensive study of the viability of the rural communes in the face of capitalist development. He concluded that market forces were leading to the breakup of the communes and the establishment of private ownership of land. As a result there was an increasing class differentiation between poor and better-off peasants. The communes were disintegrating. They could not therefore be the basis for a socialist society. Plekhanov concluded that to talk about skipping over the stage of capitalist development in Russia was ludicrous. Capitalism was becoming entrenched.

Within two years Plekhanov had become a committed Marxist. In September 1883 he and a small band of exiles formed Russia's first Marxist organisation – the Emancipation of Labour Group. This was hardly the best moment for launching a new revolutionary current. At the start of the 1880s the terrorists were at the peak of their popularity, leaving the Marxists isolated. Then after 1883 the wave of radicalisation ended, partly due to the stepped-up repression following the Tsar's assassination. But even more importantly, the political weaknesses of the populists had run the movement into the sand. The peasants to whom they looked to bring socialism had not proved a revolutionary force, and terrorist tactics had failed to overthrow the old order. The Tsar had been killed but his system continued. The universities were tamed politically and from 1881-1886 there was a low level of strikes. But even though populism and terrorism ceased to inspire large numbers, the remaining radicals were reluctant to abandon the populist ideas that had led to such heroic actions and turn instead to a totally new and politically isolated outlook – Marxism.

The leading populists were extremely hostile, condemning the Marxists as "traitors" to the revolutionary cause and denouncing them as "sectarians". The Narodniks argued that "for them [the Marxists] the polemic with Narodnaya Volya is more topical than the struggle with the Russian government and with other exploiters of the Russian people." The Emancipation of Labour Group was accused of disrupting revolutionary unity and aiding the forces of reaction. This was to become the standard attack on Marxists for their principled politics. "For the crime of insisting on theoretical clarity, for attempting to draw a clear line of demarcation between itself and other political tendencies, Marxism is always accused of the sin of 'sectarianism', of being against 'left unity.'"[20] But it is only from a firm standpoint that rejects unprincipled "unity" with forces which are not committed to working class revolution that a movement can be built that has any hope of challenging the power of capital.

Plekhanov's own forces were tiny to begin with: just five – Plekhanov himself, Axlerod, Zasulich (the one-time terrorist), Ignatov and Deutsch. They were soon reduced to three.

Deutsch was arrested in 1884 and Ignatov died in 1885. This isolation made theoretical clarity and a rock solid commitment to Marxist ideas an absolute necessity if the Group was to have any chance of laying the basis for a socialist movement.

Plekhanov proved equal to the task. But it was no simple transition. He had to go from being an activist who slept with a revolver under his pillow – an agitator, organiser, inspiring speaker and leaflet writer – to being a theoretician and propagandist developing the ideas of Marxism and writing for the tiny audience of radicals open to Marxist ideas. He had to go from being an acclaimed leader acknowledged by tens of thousands to an isolated exile arguing for highly unpopular ideas and trying to win over ones and twos. Despite the odds stacked against him, Plekhanov persisted.

During the course of the 1880s Plekhanov wrote a series of theoretical works which laid the foundations upon which a subsequent generation of Marxists was to build. He started in 1883 with *Socialism and political struggle*, a critique of populism. Then followed *Our Differences* in 1885 – a thick, heavy tome and a highly polemical work – which contained practically all the basic ideas that formed the stock-in-trade of Russian Marxism up to the end of the nineteenth century.

Plekhanov showed that, contrary to the beliefs of the populists, capitalism was transforming the Russian economy. He argued that revolutionaries had to look to the rising working class as the force to bring socialism. Plekhanov criticised the elitist conspiratorial methods of the populists – their belief that a small core of activists could carry out the revolution on behalf of the masses. He reaffirmed Marx's contention that socialism was the emancipation of the working class and had to be accomplished by the activity of the working class itself. Not all the ideas of the Group were clarified overnight. The continuing influence of populist ideas was reflected in their first draft program, which recognised "the necessity for terrorist struggle against the absolute government."[21]

Plekhanov placed great stress on the role of the socialist intelligentsia in taking socialist ideas to workers. The Group's main activity was the distribution of serious works of Marxist literature and to facilitate this, they bought their own printing press. They aimed at winning a solid base among the radical intelligentsia, who would then agitate amongst workers.[22] Cut off by the Tsarist police state and the decline of the left they had very few contacts inside Russia. They briefly made contact with a group in St Petersburg around Dimiter Blagoev – subsequently a founder of the Bulgarian Communist Party – but within a year the secret police had broken them up. Then for almost six years the Emancipation of Labour Group lost all organised contact in Russia, though unknown to them some Marxist groups did develop.[23] At the end of 1891 they made their first significant contacts. 1891-92 proved to be the beginning of a renewed upswing in struggle – the start of an unprecedented era of oppositional activity.

The Emancipation of Labour Group placed great stress on theoretical clarity. It did not easily admit new members. This, combined with Plekhanov's personal aloofness, alienated some young followers. Indeed for two decades its membership remained virtually the same. Nevertheless the breakthrough of the 1890s would hardly have been possible but for the patient, devoted and solid preparatory work of the Group. Part of the Group's historic mission lay in the creation of a theoretical and political atmosphere in radical circles that made Marxist ideas acceptable to revolutionaries. By its tireless critique of populist philosophies it eroded some of the foundations of populism and rendered it unpalatable to many in the younger generation. Marxist ideas then began to fill the vacuum.

The Marxists were aided by political developments – the failure of going to the peasantry, the greater openness of workers to socialist ideas, the failure of terrorist methods. A new generation of radicals began to see the need for a mass movement. Where was it to come from? Only the working class remained as a possible force. Even non-Marxists began to turn to workers. For some years activists adopted an eclectic approach. They accepted some Marxist ideas but held onto some populist ideas, in particular a commitment to terrorism. The gains of the Marxists were initially subterranean. But by the mid-1890s Marxism was on the march. Links were restored between the Marxist exiles and activists in Russia, as more and more young Marxists who had cut their teeth on Plekhanov's writings made their way to Geneva. In August 1900 Lenin met Plekhanov for the first time and established an at times rocky collaboration which was to lay the basis for the formation of Russia's first socialist party.

Plekhanov laid down a firm political basis which meant that the new generation of Marxists could build on a sound foundation. Lenin and Trotsky did not have to reinvent the wheel.[24] They did not have to solve every political question. And partly because of the work of the Emancipation of Labour Group, the new generation of Marxists were operating in a political environment in which core Marxist ideas were more acceptable in radical circles. Plekhanov's towering theoretical works and his popularisation of Marx's works gave the Marxist world view tremendous intellectual authority. In Russia and Eastern Europe in the course of the 1890s Marxism became a theoretical current that intellectuals of all shades had to come to grips with.

Not that Plekhanov was right on every question. He overstated the progressive role Russian capitalists would play in the revolution against Tsarism and downplayed the importance of workers operating independently of the capitalists. Nor did Plekhanov prove capable of leading a mass party, and tragically he subsequently moved to the right. In the aftermath of the 1905 revolution he declared in response to the heroic uprising of the workers of Moscow: "it was wrong to take up arms".[25] But Plekhanov's move to the right does not mean we should undervalue the role he played in an earlier period – thirty years of tremendously productive revolutionary activity.

There are important lessons from Plekhanov's career for today. Socialist Alternative currently only has several hundred members. It can seem there is an almost unbridgeable gulf between our puny forces and the task we have set ourselves – building a party that can lead the working class to power. But if we are small, spare a thought for Plekhanov in

1885 with only three members. For its first ten years the Emancipation of Labour Group had to fight a thankless struggle against the stream, while being denounced by the rest of the left as "sectarians" and "splitters". Yet the Group's persistence, their adherence to revolutionary principle, their hard headed approach and their realistic perspective meant that they were able to lay the basis for a party that did indeed lead the working class to power. But at first that simply meant winning over individuals.

Some people on the left argue that it is impossible for a socialist propaganda group to transform itself into a mass party. But that is precisely what did happen in Russia. Plekhanov showed it could be done. And the Russian example is far from being the only one. The same pattern was followed in country after country. We can't lay out in advance the road by which a mass socialist party will be built in Australia, or how long it will take. Nor are we arguing that a mass party will be built simply by arithmetical recruitment to Socialist Alternative. Other revolutionary currents can emerge that will be part of that process. It will depend in large part upon political developments that are beyond our control. But there are some things we do have control over.

Clearly there are massive differences between semi-feudal Russia, where workers were only beginning to emerge as a class, and an advanced capitalist country where the working class is the overwhelming majority of the population and has a long history of union and political organisation. Nor is there currently in Australia a substantial layer of radical intellectuals as there was in Russia. So I'm not advocating that socialists rush out to buy a printing press and focus on churning out thick books polemicising against the ALP and Greens (though a few more serious books on these questions would hardly go astray). Nevertheless, many of our tasks are similar to those that confronted Plekhanov. True, we don't have the task of developing a totally new Marxist tradition and applying it to Australian conditions. Much of that work has been done. The core ideas of Marxism have been developed by those revolutionaries who have gone before us. Nevertheless socialists today in many ways are also pioneers. We are confronted with the question of rebuilding the socialist movement and the broader workers' movement after a long period of retreat.

This is not going to be accomplished overnight. To achieve it will take a persistent commitment to revolutionary principles and a realistic perspective, which were key characteristics of the Emancipation of Labour Group. The essential task today is cohering the initial forces from the radical minority that does exist – what might be termed "the primitive accumulation of cadres". Such a layer of socialist activists will be decisive for rebuilding a militant left-wing current in the trade unions and the student movement.

CHAPTER FOUR

The rise of Marxism in Poland

The Polish socialist movement dates from the late 1870s.[26] In the late nineteenth century the part of Poland occupied by Russia was the most industrially advanced section of the Tsarist Empire and consequently it was here that a labour movement first arose. The Polish socialist movement soon divided into two currents. A nationalist current coalesced as the Polish Socialist Party (PPS. It saw the struggle for Polish independence as its central task and put off the struggle for socialism until a vague, indefinite future. Opposed to the reformist PPS was an internationalist Marxist current arguing for the unity of all workers of the Tsarist Empire. The Polish Marxists, who included Rosa Luxemburg and Leo Jogiches, formed the Social Democratic Party of the Kingdom of Poland (SDKP in 1893.

The SDKP grew to about 400 members – predominantly high school and university students – before being virtually destroyed by police repression in 1895. From then on Luxemburg and Jogiches as émigrés had little direct involvement in building the movement on the ground in Poland. But they still set the theoretical tone, which was one of strident opposition to Polish nationalism This became *the* defining issue. It was reflected in bitter hostility to the reformist PPS. SDKP publications were noted for their sharp polemical tone. It also led to bitter polemics with Lenin who supported the right of national self-determination for Poland and to a walk-out by the Polish Marxists from the founding conference of the Russian Social Democratic Labour Party (SDLP).[27]

Jogiches and Luxemburg are much more famous, but the success of the Polish Marxists on the ground owes much to Feliks Dzierzynski. Dzierzynski, a Pole from Lithuania, became politically active at high school. In 1895, aged just 18, he was directing his own student circle and helped form an internationalist left in the Lithuanian Social Democratic Party (LSDP). Dzierzynski was no theoretician to rival Luxemburg. As another prominent Polish Marxist Adolf Warski wrote: "Ideas for Dzierzynski existed in order to translate them into action, in order to fight for them, in order to bring them to life."[28]

In July 1897 Dzierzynski was arrested – the first of many, many arrests. In 1899 he escaped from Siberia – the first of many such escapes. In his absence the LSDP had been shattered by repression, so he went to Warsaw, the capital of Poland. There was only a small remnant left of the SDKP in Warsaw, so Dzierzynski joined the PPS. It was a straight-out entry job. Dzierzynski had nothing but contempt for the PPS's reformist politics. He attacked the PPS for its nationalism and downplaying of workers' class demands. He found support among artisanal workers – shoemakers, bakers and hairdressers. By November 1899 he had organised 200 workers in Marxist circles and formed the Social Democratic Party of the Kingdom of Poland and Lithuania (SDKPiL). He was arrested in February 1900 but left behind a nucleus of dedicated young activists – more than half the members were aged 18-25. The emergence of this core of activists trained by Dzierzynski meant the party did not collapse in the face of repression as it had in 1895-1896. Indeed, by 1901 it had grown to over 1,000 members.

After two years in Siberia Dzierzynski escaped. By then the SDKPiL had been weakened by further police attacks and internal disagreements. Dzierzynski, in alliance with Jogiches and Luxemburg, quickly reasserted his authority. He based himself in Cracow in Austrian-ruled Poland, where there was less police repression.

Students (both university and high school) were far and away "the most politicised social group in Polish society on the eve of the 1904 Russo-Japanese war". The leading activists of both the SDKPiL and the PPS were mainly students. "Of 56 persons arrested in a Warsaw funeral demonstration organised by the SDKPiL in May (1904), 34 were students or former students and only two could be classified as workers."[29] The entire southern committee of the SDKPiL consisted of students from the Institute of Agriculture and Forestry. At the start of 1904 the SDKPiL had 125-150 members in Warsaw loosely organised in propaganda circles.[30] Its rival the PPS was five times larger. But the SDKPiL had the advantage of greater ideological unity.[31]

Dzierzynski introduced more conspiratorial methods to reduce arrests and removed some elements inclined to engage in terrorism. He developed an elaborate system of underground agents sent across the border from Cracow. In the course of 1904 the SDKPiL "transformed itself from a loose and highly vulnerable network of circles into a tightly controlled, centrally directed and far more disciplined organisation" with the beginnings of a working class membership.[32] This meant they were well placed to intervene in a decisive development – the revolutionary wave that swept the Tsarist Empire in 1905.

The outbreak of the Russo-Japanese war led to economic crisis – a sharp rise in unemployment and inflation – and in turn rising discontent. The PPS split. Its émigré leadership was stridently nationalist and its main leader, Josef Pilsudski, went to Tokyo to negotiate a military alliance with Japan. However in Poland younger PPS members were less nationalist and emphasised working class struggle. This created more space for the SDKPiL. It went from being one-fifth the size of the PPS to two-thirds its size by the end of 1904. It took a very hard line on the PPS and if anything was sectarian to the emerging PPS left.

The Bloody Sunday massacre in St Petersburg in January 1905 sparked a massive upsurge of struggle. A general strike erupted in Warsaw and the class struggle was to reach a higher pitch in Poland than in any other part of the Tsarist Empire. The SDKPiL burst into activity and was prominent in workers' struggles. It also backed the mass student campaign for Polish national rights. The Polish Marxists took a more nuanced line on the national question than might have been expected. They called for the equality of nationalities in the Tsarist Empire, with freedom of cultural development, national schools and national autonomy for Poland.

Dzierzynski also moderated the tone of the SDKPiL's polemics against the PPS left. So some of the sectarian edges were taken off the organisation as it developed in the course of the mass struggle. Though not all: the only trade unions they would support were ones made up exclusively of SDKPiL members. This line was endorsed by Luxemburg, who seems to have concluded from her clashes with the reformist trade union leaders in Germany that any union not led by Marxists was an obstacle to the class struggle. At the height of the 1905 revolt this sectarian position on the unions did not particularly hurt the SDKPiL. It did, however, become a serious problem after the defeat of the revolution.

In the first months of 1905, confronted by the challenges of revolutionary mass politics, this lean, conspiratorial organisation found itself in danger of "losing its head and bursting open" in the words of Dzierzynski, who now called for greater autonomy to local organisations. Party resources were overwhelmed by the membership growth. There was a shortage of literature and trained agitators. Dzierzynski declared: "absolutely everyone is exhausted."[33]

The newness of the organisation led to mistakes. At times the SDKPiL succumbed to pressure for premature action. In one case student members encouraged an abortive uprising by soldiers in the south of Poland. But the party had a genuine vitality. Despite large-scale arrests of party activists in March 1905, the SDKPiL quickly recovered and continued to grow. On May Day 1905 the SDKPiL mobilised a 30,000-strong contingent in Warsaw. Troops opened fire on them, leaving 50 dead and 100 wounded. In response the SDKPiL called for a general strike, but it failed. Luxemburg and Jogiches became worried that the leadership was on an adventurist course but after talks with Dzierzynski the party managed to reorient.

The SDKPiL was forced to break its conspiratorial cover to relate to the mass movement. This led to the arrest of Dzierzynski and the rest of the Warsaw leadership. Nevertheless, by the last months of 1906 they had grown to 40,000 – only slightly smaller than the PPS. So in the space of three short years they had gone from being a small propaganda group of at best a couple of hundred members to being a real force in the working class. By early 1907 in the textile centre of Lodz alone, they had 20,000 members. They had established a mass party that united Polish, German and Jewish workers. Their mass following was confirmed by the fact that the SDKPiL got 68 per cent of the working class vote in the Duma elections in Lodz.

In December 1906 the bosses went on the offensive and locked out the militant workers of Lodz for 20 weeks. Despite bitter street-fighting the capitalists reasserted their control. After this defeat the workers' movement began to decline. The scale of repression in Poland was more severe than in any other part of the Tsarist Empire. Between January 1908 and October 1909 10,000 militants were exiled to Siberia from Lodz alone, a city of about 400,000.[34] The SDKPiL was broken. By 1910 it had fewer than 1,000 members. As for Dzierzynski, after a series of further arrests and escapes, he was jailed in 1912 and not freed until the February 1917 revolution in Russia. He was then elected to the executive of the Moscow Soviet and to the Bolshevik Central Committee in July 1917. After the October revolution he headed the Cheka, the Soviet intelligence organisation.

Lessons for today

What are we to conclude from all this? Firstly, that it is possible in the right circumstances for a socialist propaganda group to transform itself into a mass party. The SDKPiL was able to do so in an extremely short period of time, partly because of the scale of the revolutionary upheaval in 1905, and because Poland did not have an entrenched reformist labour movement. We are much less likely to see quite such dramatic growth in more advanced capitalist societies with established political and union traditions. Nevertheless the pattern of all Marxist organisations tends to be one of rapid recruitment, during favourable times of sharp radicalisation, followed by periods of consolidation or retreat. There is no reason why Marxists in the future cannot repeat this pattern, provided they are clear and firm on their politics and on what they are doing to build their organisation.

The second conclusion then is the necessity of having a clear political line. Without that you are building on sand and cannot cohere a cadre. It was the SDKPiL's clarity on the question of working class unity and opposition to Polish nationalism that gave it a decisive advantage over its reformist rival. Of course an emphasis on political clarity and polemics with your opponents can have serious overheads. It can lead to a rigid, sectarian approach which makes the organisation incapable of adapting to new circumstances. The SDKPiL's virulent opposition to Polish nationalism led it into the error of opposing the right of national self-determination of the oppressed Polish people. If it had adhered to this orientation in the face of the enormous movement for liberation from the Russian yoke that swept Poland in 1905, the Polish Marxists would have been left isolated. However in practice they proved capable of responding to the movement.

One of the key advantages of having a clear political position is that it can be argued against, modified and corrected. You can't do that with a fudged position. You can't educate a cadre around confusion. Nor can you build cadre in the abstract simply by reading books, though reading is, of course, vital. You can't build a cadre separately from confronting the issues and tasks necessary to build a revolutionary organisation, whatever its size, at any particular point of time.

The third conclusion is on the role of students. Student revolutionaries played a vital role in building the SDKPiL into a mass working-class party. This pattern has been replicated on dozens of occasions, from China to Iraq to Bulgaria to Vietnam to Sri Lanka to Japan. The social differences between students and workers in Poland in 1904 were very much greater than in Australia today. Students were an absolutely tiny proportion of the population and considerably more privileged. Yet the Polish student Marxists were able to reach out to workers. It can be done again. The fact that Socialist Alternative's membership today is predominantly student and ex-student is nothing to apologise for. It is an entirely necessary stage Marxists often have to go through to achieve our ultimate objective of building a mass working-class party.

There is a final point. Political clarity is vital, but on its own it is far from sufficient. One of the key reasons that the young revolutionaries of the SDKPiL were able to build was because, fired by a deep commitment to Marxist ideals, they were extremely dedicated, persevering and prepared to take risks and make sacrifices. Feliks Dzierzynski had all these qualities in abundance. As his biographer Robert Blobaum put it: "Dzierzynski was a thoroughly dedicated party activist willing to take on any task no matter how difficult, and use any means at his disposal to promote and defend 'the cause' of revolution."[35] Any serious socialist organisation needs many more such comrades.

CHAPTER FIVE

Early French Communism

In December 1920 at the Congress of Tours, the French Socialist Party (SP) voted overwhelmingly to join the Communist International (Comintern) – the international revolutionary movement founded in the wake of the 1917 Russian revolution by the Bolsheviks.[36] A reformist minority refused to accept the decision and split away, but the new French Communist Party (PCF) outnumbered them by 110,000 to 30,000. The Communists had the support of the party's youth wing and controlled the daily paper *L'Humanité* with a paid sale of 200,000. The mood of PCF activists was euphoric. France seemed ripe for revolutionary action.

A tiny handful of socialists played a decisive role in establishing this mass party. However you can only understand their success by taking into account two key objective factors: World War I and the Russian revolution. The war had a traumatic impact on French workers and peasants. Out of a population of 40 million, five million were killed or wounded. The devastation led to a revolutionary mood across Europe which was sharpened by the Russian revolution. It gave hope to tens of millions. Another world seemed truly possible.

The old French left was totally discredited by the war, which it backed virtually unanimously. The pre-war left had two main currents. First there was the SP. Despite its radical rhetoric it was essentially reformist and nationalist. It focused on parliament and had no base in the unions. The other current was the syndicalists who controlled the union federation, the General Confederation of Labour (CGT). In their early years the syndicalists looked to revolutionary unions to overthrow capitalism. They dismissed the SP as middle class and reformist. But in the years immediately before the war the syndicalists moved in a reformist direction themselves. Then at the start of the war in August 1914 the CGT agreed to discipline workers to work harder for the war effort. Meanwhile the SP entered the war cabinet.[37]

It was not until the end of October 1914 that a tiny group of internationalists began to meet in Paris. It is important to understand just how isolated these opponents of the war were. Pro-war nationalism in France was even stronger than in Germany. The German Social Democratic Party (SPD supported the war but one revolutionary MP, Karl Liebknecht, heroically spoke out and provided a focus for anti-war sentiment. Nothing like that happened in France. In Germany the prominent revolutionary Rosa Luxemburg had a circle of supporters with a Marxist understanding of imperialism. Luxemburg is often criticised for not breaking earlier with the reformist SPD to form a party on Bolshevik lines.[38] But at least they were not starting entirely from scratch in Germany. Luxemburg and her supporters provided the kernel around which a Communist Party eventually cohered.

In France the revolutionaries were starting from *behind* scratch. There was absolutely no French Marxist opposition. Virtually no one in France was clear on imperialism, no one was clear on the need for a revolutionary party, let alone on how such a party was to be built. A motley collection first came together to oppose the war. It included the syndicalists Alfred Rosmer and Pierre Monatte, a few SP members and some anarchists. The only Marxists involved were a group of Russian exiles which included Leon Trotsky. Initially this loose group held weekly discussion meetings to clarify their ideas. Their first open act came in December 1914 when Monatte publicly resigned from the CGT leadership in opposition to its support for the war. The government's response was to draft him into the army. In August 1915 the Teachers' Federation began to criticise the war. They had a pacifist position, not a revolutionary anti-imperialist position like Luxemburg and Lenin's Bolsheviks. Nonetheless teacher activists, most notably Ferdinand Loriot, played a prominent role in forming the PCF.

In the first five months of the war 300,000 French soldiers died. In the face of this slaughter, unease emerged in SP ranks. But even after a year of war this opposition remained underconfident and far from clear politically. Some Socialist MPs moved to a semi-pacifist position. But they were very concerned to be respectable and not undermine party unity, and they continued to vote in parliament to fund the war effort.

The Zimmerwald conference of anti-war socialists in Switzerland in September 1915 galvanized the dispersed elements of opposition. It gave them a rallying cry, the skeleton of a program and above all the assurance that they were not alone. Zimmerwald was divided between revolutionaries like the Bolsheviks and moderate socialists who came to be known as centrists. The motions adopted at Zimmerwald were a compromise, but they did push the socialist movement to the left.

In January 1916 the Committee for the Resumption of International Relations (with socialists in other countries) was formed in Paris. It brought together socialists, syndicalists, anarchists and exiled Russian Marxists such as Trotsky. This was the tiny acorn from which the PCF grew. It was a more formal group and issued membership cards. But political conditions remained extremely difficult. Anti-war socialists were harassed on all sides. The government banned their meetings and sent spies into their midst. Yet they persisted and began very gradually to make ground.

To build on firm foundations there needed to be ideological clarification. It was not sufficient just to oppose the war. All the rotten traditions of the French left had to be confronted – the nationalism, the reliance on parliament, the confusion about the role of the unions. Without such a clarification no Communist Party could have been formed. The Russian Marxists, who published their own paper in Paris, *Nashe Slovo*, played an important role in this process of political clarification. Trotsky was expelled from France in September 1916 but he had made an impact on some of the leading comrades who were to form the PCF.

May 1917 saw strikes by metalworkers in Paris. In June the strike wave grew among munitions workers and miners. Strike demonstrations often turned into protests against the war. 1917 also saw a wave of mutinies in the army. In some cases the troops elected soldiers' councils and attempted to march on Paris. But despite this shift in the political climate at the October 1917 SP Congress the far left was isolated; though among the syndicalists a new radical current emerged. Some strikes in 1918 saw workers seize control of factories and entire towns. But the strikes were suppressed, the leaders arrested and sent to the front. By the northern spring of 1919 the SP and CGT policy of class collaboration was seen as a terrible mistake. With the end of the war both the CGT and SP were flooded with new members. 1.5 million joined the CGT. 1919 and 1920 saw upheavals of revolutionary proportions. Enthusiasm for the Russian revolution grew. One worker commented:

> I know nothing of Bolshevism. I have neither the leisure or the means to study it. But my landlord, my boss, and my neighbour – each of whom is more greedy and reactionary than the next – speak badly of it. Therefore it must be doing something worthwhile.[39]

The SP grew from 34,000 in 1918 to 180,000 in December 1920. The new recruits by and large were radical. They hated the war and were hostile to the old leaders who had pledged the party to the war effort. "They returned from the great slaughter mutilated or bruised...They blamed the regime...and they wanted to overthrow it."[40] However at the April 1919 SP Congress the new militants were still disorganised, so the centrists dominated. The far-left minority led by Loriot which called for support for the newly formed Comintern got just 270 votes out of over 2000.

Among the far left there was widespread confusion as to the real nature of Bolshevism. Numerous currents, including even anarchists, embraced the Bolsheviks as "theirs". In part this was due to lack of information because of the censorship and imperialist blockade of Russia.

The organised Marxist forces were still miniscule. According to a police report a February 1919 meeting of the Committee for Resumption of International Relations attracted just 20 people.[41] In May 1919 they formed the Committee for the Third International. Initially it included syndicalists and anarchists. The anarchists were for splitting immediately from the SP. They formed their own short-lived Communist Party. A group of revolutionary syndicalists organised an opposition in the CGT and unlike in the past they worked with the revolutionary forces in the SP. So the best of the syndicalists had shifted politically, partly because of Trotsky's influence. But they did not completely abandon syndicalism. They saw the Russian soviets as being like revolutionary unions.

The struggle against centrism

During the course of 1919 new forces joined the Committee for the Third International. Some were young intellectuals new to politics, like Boris Souvarine. Others were older SP members who had been pulled to the left. Even the centrist leaders were moving towards the Comintern. Souvarine pressed to break with the SP. But Loriot and Monatte opposed a premature split. They were proved correct by the February 1920 SP Congress, where for the first time the revolutionary left offered a real challenge. In the key federation of the Seine – the area around Paris – Loriot won a large majority for affiliation to the Comintern. However the left was still not clear on what it wanted. It was united more by hostility to the right than by a clear Marxist program. In March 1920 reliable communications were established with the Bolsheviks. With the help of a Russian subsidy the left began to publish a weekly journal and stepped up its polemics against the centrists.

The northern spring of 1920 saw a major rail strike which turned into a generalised stoppage. The strike was initiated by syndicalists with visions of a spontaneous revolution. But it ended in a bad defeat. This rammed home the lesson that what was needed was a revolutionary party to cohere and give a decisive lead to the militants who wanted to overturn the system. Capitalism was not going to overthrown simply by some elemental rebellion from below. For there to be any hope of victory, there had to be a clear and well-organised revolutionary leadership that had broken decisively from the reformists.

A variety of forces began to grope towards this understanding. Two centrist leaders, Cachin and Frossard, went to Moscow to negotiate with the Bolsheviks. Frossard had been a moderate during the war; Cachin strongly pro-war. But both were moving left – otherwise they would have lost all rank and file support in the SP. On their return they argued to join the Comintern. But they were still far from being committed Leninists. The decision on whether to join was to be made at the Tours Congress which opened on 25 December 1920. The vote to join was an overwhelming 3,208 to 1,022. The new PCF had 110,000 members, but this was a loose membership and hardly fully communist.

A period of political clarification, education and practical experience was going to be necessary. But who was to do the educating? The leaders of the left, like Loriot and Souvarine, were a minority in a leadership headed by centrists like Cachin and Frossard.

Some of the most determined revolutionary activists, such as Monatte, had not entirely broken with their syndicalist prejudices and were not yet party members.

Frossard and Cachin did not give a decisive lead. They aimed to hang on to power rather than argue for a Marxist road forward. They made concessions to the right wing of the PCF that had not liked breaking with the reformists. They also made concessions to the syndicalists over work in the unions. The syndicalists, who included many PCF members, demanded that the PCF not organise in the unions as a disciplined body with its own democratically determined political line. As a consequence there were three left factions inside the CGT – revolutionary syndicalists, communists and pure syndicalists. All three factions were led by PCF members!

The lack of a clear Marxist leadership meant that the PCF was a confused mish-mash. In Paris and among the youth there was a strong ultraleft sentiment. As a result of this irresolute leadership, by March 1922 membership had fallen to 60,000. The Bolsheviks intervened to try to straighten things out. But it is no easy task to create a revolutionary party almost from scratch, and as Trotsky explained, if the Bolsheviks had pushed ahead too sharply, almost everything could have been lost:

> [T]he Frossard group gave good reasons for us to break with them. But, at the time, the rupture would not have been understood by the great majority of the membership ... the new split would have taken place on a chance basis and the International would have regrouped in the left a disparate group itself needing to be weeded out. It was necessary, therefore, to give the left elements the time to see their tasks clearly, to acquire ideological cohesion and to bring around themselves a large number of party members – and it was only after this that the ideological, critical and educative work of the International could be finished off by big and energetic organisational measures having a "surgical" character.[42]

Not that everything was going badly. In December 1921 the CGT split. The PCF and the more sensible syndicalists opposed the split, which was led by ultraleft anarchists. Nevertheless the radical breakaway, the CGTU, was larger than the reformist CGT, and a strong current hostile to the CGTU's sectarian anarchist leadership soon cohered.

In December 1922 Frossard, under pressure from the Comintern, resigned from the PCF and the left took over the leadership. Though Frossard took with him "most of the 'politicians', journalists, municipal councillors and the like", the bulk of the worker membership remained loyal.[43] Here was a real chance to transform the PCF into a genuine Bolshevik party. But the problems were far from solved. The left was not a cohesive group capable of providing astute leadership.

Souvarine and another key left leader, Albert Treint, were at loggerheads. Treint was crude politically, had no idea how to apply the united front policy with the reformist organisations and was authoritarian in his organisational methods. Souvarine was more correct politically but often behaved in an undisciplined fashion. The lesson here is that it is very difficult to cohere a Marxist leadership in a few years of upheaval. The quieter times before great outbursts of struggle are vital for training the core of a future mass party. It is in this period that leaders can be tested. A tradition of democratic collective leadership based on open debate of political differences and working together as a self-disciplined team that complements each individual leader's strengths and weaknesses can be established.

The Bolsheviks were desperate to spread the revolution. They had no alternative but to attempt to create Communist parties in the West at a forced march. But there were overheads. A mechanical selection of leaders was taking place. A leadership team had not coalesced in the PCF which had learnt to work collaboratively together over a period of years without blow-ups over secondary issues or debilitating personal squabbles. Nevertheless there was some progress. The PCF passed the test of the French military occupation of the German Ruhr in January 1923. Unlike the old SP it took a firm anti-imperialist position and solidarised with the struggles of the German workers. By the end of 1923 the best of the syndicalists had joined the party and become part of the leadership. The PCF now controlled the CGTU with its 400,000 members. In July 1923 the PCF won control of the left-wing war veterans' association and it was beginning to recruit some prominent intellectuals. In the May 1924 elections the PCF managed to win 26 seats.[44]

Problems undoubtedly remained – continuing sectarianism and a strong tendency towards over-centralisation. But these could have been ironed out. The party still had 50,000 members compared to the SP's 49,000. But in 1924 the Stalinist degeneration of the Russian revolution began to have a dramatic impact. The PCF leadership rightly refused to condemn Trotsky. That led to a Moscow organised purge of the most able leaders – Monatte, Rosmer, Loriot and Souvarine. It was the end of any hope of forming a genuinely revolutionary party.

To conclude

Mass revolutionary parties don't come out of nowhere. They have to be built by real people. Initially that usually means handfuls of activists. Of course a mass party can't be decreed by an act of will. The devastation of World War I and the inspiration of the Russian Revolution created the mass sentiment out of which the PCF could be built. But without the tireless work of the tiny group of socialists organised in the Committee for the Third International, there would have been no mass Communist Party founded in December 1920. So small groups of socialists can make a real difference. The tragedy in France was that a group of Marxists had not come together five years earlier so that they could have clarified their ideas and learnt to work together *before* the great challenges posed by war and revolution. Even if there had been ten organised Marxists in Paris in 1914, some of the most elementary mistakes made by the early PCF could potentially have been avoided, and possibly a party could have been formed before the revolutionary wave peaked in 1920. We can't rewind the film of history. What we can do is to try not to commit the same mistakes. The extent to which socialists build now, when there are not surging masses in the streets, can be decisive.

CHAPTER SIX

The origins of communism in China

The Chinese Communist Party (CCP) was a direct product of the intellectual ferment that accompanied the anti-imperialist demonstrations and strikes of 1919 – the May Fourth Movement. Prior to 1919 "not a single figure emerged who could even be remotely identified as a Marxist."[45] Indeed, China lacked even a reformist social democratic tradition. The May Fourth Movement erupted in opposition to the Versailles agreement that ceded the former German imperial concessions in China to Japan. Starting with mass student protests in Beijing, the movement spread rapidly. At its height it saw China's first general strike – 100,000 workers struck in the industrial centre of Shanghai. "This largely spontaneous action...alerted radical intellectuals to the political potential of labour...they threw themselves into the business of educating and organizing labour."[46] Capitalism had clearly arrived in China and for the newly radicalised students who led the movement the question of class was seen as central.

A layer of young educated activists turned to Marxism in the wake of the May Fourth Movement – a diffuse political and culturally radical movement strongly influenced by anarchism. In December 1919 Chen Duxiu, one of China's leading intellectuals and the future CCP general secretary, proclaimed that the task was to create a society that was "sincere, progressive, activist, free, egalitarian, creative, beautiful, kind, peaceful, full of universal love, mutual assistance, pleasant labour and prosperous for all".[47]

Numerous study societies were set up. "Many of China's later communist leaders were schooled in groups such as the 'New People's Study Society,' the 'Awakening Society,' and the 'Social Welfare society'."[48] These study circles were vital for debating out and clarifying the ideas of the student activists. They were the basis on which a mass socialist movement was built in the space of a few short years, almost entirely from scratch. As S.A. Smith writes in his inspiring account of the early Communist movement in Shanghai:

> The students, teachers, journalists and others who gave ideological and organizational direction to the boycotts and strikes combined a passionate commitment to individual liberation with root-and-branch rejection of traditional values and institutions and a yearning for the radical reconstruction of society on the basis of democracy and equality.[49]

Numerous anarchist-inspired communes were formed to help establish this new society. However by 1920 "the radical fervor of the May Fourth Movement had given way to disillusionment. The mass movement had receded...The communal movement...had run into grave difficulties." "The Communist movement...got under way...at a moment of crisis in Chinese radicalism, when the ideological and organisational premises that had informed radical activity during the preceding years seemed to have run into a dead end."[50]

The most radical students and intellectuals were looking for new answers after the failure of their communal experiments which showed the limits class society imposed on individual activity. This made them receptive to the arguments of the Comintern agent, the Russian revolutionary Grigirii Voitinskii, that class struggle was the way to change the world and that they should follow the successful example of the Russian revolution by forming a Bolshevik-style party.

With the encouragement of Voitinskii, who arrived in China in the northern spring of 1920, Chen Duxiu set up the Marxist Research Society in Shanghai in May 1920. Though it had just fourteen members – all intellectuals – it formed the basis of the CCP. Marxist study circles were established in a number of urban centres. The Shanghai group was instrumental in the establishment of groups in Wuhan, Jinan, Changsha and Guangzhou. At Beijing University Li Dazhao, the other dominant intellectual figure in the young CCP, established a study circle which introduced many of the subsequent leaders of the CCP to Marxism.

There was a sharp cultural divide between the young student activists and the mass of workers. It was not simply the students' higher level of education, but also the fact that they adopted Western dress and were culturally Westernised. Nevertheless they were able to win a working class audience. Party membership made heavy demands on these young intellectuals, requiring them to forego the possibility of a conventional career and to subordinate their life to the cause of working class self-emancipation. For many it demanded the ultimate sacrifice at the hands of the defenders of capitalist "civilisation". But in return it provided them with a deeper meaning in life and a chance to achieve personal fulfilment in the struggle to liberate humanity.

In August 1920 a Socialist Youth League (SYL was formed in Shanghai. It soon grew to thirty members, mostly students. These socialist activists were young, inexperienced and often had romantic ideas. But they were the most serious students of their generation. They wanted to do something, not just talk. Nevertheless they had only a very limited understanding of Marxism and had not fully broken with the individualist, idealist and emotional style of politics typical of anarcho-communism. So there were numerous arguments about the need for a centralised and disciplined organisation. Initially you did not have to be a Marxist to join the SYL and there were numerous anarchists in it. It was not until the Second CCP Congress in 1922 that the break with anarchism was complete.

Unlike the Communist parties formed in some Western European countries after the Russian revolution – parties organised on the basis of left-wing splits from the old social democratic parties – China's total lack of a social democratic tradition meant there was no layer of experienced cadre versed in at least the basic ideas of Marxism to provide the core of the CCP. A Marxist cadre had to be tempered and educated from a layer of young activists with virtually no political traditions. Comintern agents played a vital role in cohering these inexperienced radicals and giving them a clear direction and program.

In these first few years many CCP members, including leading comrades like Chen Duxiu, were still influenced by anarchist and reformist ideas. A sharp boundary had to be established between the political approach of communists and their ideological competitors on the left – anarchists and to a lesser extent reformist socialists. The CCP debated the differences between Marxism, anarchism and guild socialism in order to educate its members in revolutionary politics and to achieve organisational and ideological coherence. In the course of these debates a sorting-out occurred. Some prominent founding members, who had an academic attraction to Marxism or who wanted to establish careers in bourgeois society, dropped out as they could not make the transition to Bolshevism; whereas a number of younger student comrades came to the fore.

The new CCP saw its paramount task as labour organisation. It set up workers' schools to make contact with worker activists. The schools were used to form workers' clubs which in turn helped build factory cells and provided the nucleus for unions.

> Although the precise structure...varied from place to place...the communist organizations functioned in a three-fold structure. Operating illegally at the core were the communist small groups; then there were units of the Socialist Youth Corps operating semi-openly and providing a recruitment pool for the party; and finally the Marxist study societies presented a public face, trying to reach the widest possible audience.[51]

At its founding Congress in July 1921 the CCP had a mere 53 members, with another 350 in the youth group. It based itself on a clear-cut call for workers' revolution in China. However some delegates were hesitant about forming a Communist Party and/or reluctant to break with the bourgeois nationalists of the Guomindang (GMD). The CCP's attitude to the GMD emerged as a running sore, especially with the increasing Stalinisation of the Comintern.

Party work was slow in getting off the ground because of differences of opinion and financial difficulties. "A truly stable party organization was not established until the second congress in July 1922".[52] By June 1922 the CCP still only had 195 members, just twenty one of whom were workers.

The Hong Kong Seamen's strike which broke out in the early months of 1922 was to be the largest working-class mobilisation in the history of modern China to that time.

While Communist activists certainly drew inspiration from the strike, the new party was in no position to have any impact on the direction of the struggle, as it had no organised presence in Hong Kong, and in the neighbouring Guangdong province the CCP had a mere 32 members in June 1922.[53] Shanghai also saw a wave of worker militancy in 1922 which the young CCP tried to relate to. But again its small size – by the summer of 1923 it had only 53 members in the Shanghai region – limited its success.

The youth movement was more successful. By May 1922 the SYL had 200 members in Shanghai, with a large presence at Shanghai University. A breakthrough came with the launching of a nationwide anti-Christian movement in 1922. Hostility to Christianity was strong among radical youth who attacked the churches as agents for the imperialist plunder of China and propagandists for capitalism. The CCP also campaigned for women's liberation – the subordination of women was seen by Marxists as a keystone of feudal backwardness.

Until 1926 the CCP largely remained a party of the educated, though the proportion of workers slowly grew. In May 1924 of 47 members in Shanghai, 23 were teachers, journalists or other professionals, 13 were students, 8 workers and 3 merchants. By early 1925 it was estimated that 30 per cent of the 1,000 members and 9,000 youth group members were workers but a large percentage of these were unemployed or in irregular employment. The party's main base in Shanghai was at Shanghai University where the SYL had 77 members. Communists dominated the student union, which was the key centre of student radicalism in 1922-1923.

The Chinese revolution of 1925-27

In February 1925 strikes broke out in Shanghai's Japanese-owned cotton mills over the terrible working conditions and brutal management. At its peak 30,000 workers struck. Communist students helped provide leadership to the strike. More than fifty strikers joined the CCP. By May 1925 it had 220 members in Shanghai. On 30 May police shot and killed 17 students and workers who had infiltrated Shanghai's imperialist-controlled International Settlement to hand out leaflets. This sparked mass protests and strikes by over 200,000 workers – the May Thirtieth Movement. Radical anti-imperialist nationalism acquired a mass base. The renamed Communist Youth League (CYL sprang to prominence in the student movement and grew to 2,285.

Despite savage repression, the CCP-led General Labour Union grew massively. The CCP established a sizeable working class base in Shanghai. By April 1926 it had 2,500 members – over half of whom were workers. The Shanghai regional committee was hard pressed to cope with the upsurge of struggle and the influx of new members, the overwhelming majority of whom were illiterate. The membership was very young, for example the CCP head of the cotton union federation, Zhang Zuochen, was just 21 when he was executed by the GMD in June 1927.

The impact of the May Thirtieth Movement spread well beyond Shanghai. It sparked the historic Guangzhou (Canton)-Hong Kong strike which saw hundreds of thousands of workers and students abandon Hong Kong for Guangzhou and maintain a mass strike/boycott of the vital British imperialist outpost for an amazing 16 months. Despite its tiny size – "less than ten local CCP members and thirty CYL members in Hong Kong" – the CCP, with support from its larger branches in Guangzhou, assumed the leadership of the strike from the beginning.[54] The CCP grew rapidly out of the strike/boycott – from a combined total of 700 party and youth league members in Guangdong province just before the strike to more than 7,000 by its end. However the chaotic conditions of the strike/boycott, the lack of cadre and the acutely stretched party resources made it difficult to politically integrate and train the mass of new worker members, who had no previous experience of socialist politics.

The summer of 1926 saw a further wave of strikes and lockouts in Shanghai that reached revolutionary proportions. The advance of the GMD army on Shanghai provoked workers' insurrections to overthrow the local warlords, who ruled the city in alliance with the imperialist forces. The CCP played a pivotal role and grew rapidly. By April 1927 it had 57,967 members – half of whom were workers. In Shanghai membership peaked at about 10,000, with another 2,000 in the CYL.

This was an amazing achievement by the small band of student radicals that had founded the CCP in 1921. In the space of just six years they had gone from Marxist discussion circles of a few hundred students to a mass party that played a leading role in a tremendous workers' revolution. And they had done it in the extremely difficult conditions of brutal repression and economic backwardness. They proved that it was possible to build a mass Communist Party from the tiny beginnings of a small propaganda group of student radicals with literally no previous experience of Marxism. If it could be done once it can be done again. Of course the ground had been prepared for the young Chinese Communists by the political chaos and social disintegration that gripped China in these years. But similar capitalist crises in the future will again open up these sorts of opportunities. In any case, a deep social crisis only creates the *opportunity* for revolutionaries to build rapidly. For that opportunity to be realised there have to be conscious revolutionary actors who have the political understanding, the boldness and the dedication to shake the system to its foundations.

Unfortunately between April and December 1927 the tremendous opportunities that were opened up by the first Chinese revolution were snuffed out. The revolutionary workers' movement was crushed by murderous repression unleashed by the Guomindang. Up to 2,000 Communists and worker militants were murdered in Shanghai and thousands more arrested or fired from their jobs.[55]

The CCP was pulverised by this counter-revolutionary onslaught, for which it was totally unprepared, thanks to the appalling advice provided by the Stalinised Comintern. Rather than arguing that only the working class could lead a decisive struggle against imperialism and warning the young CCP of the treacherous role that the bourgeois nationalists of the Guomindang were bound to play, Stalin argued for the CCP to ally with, indeed subordinate itself to, the Guomindang.[56] But it was by studying the painful lessons of this defeat that a subsequent generation of revolutionaries, both in China and internationally, obtained an understanding of the thoroughly counter-revolutionary nature of Stalinism and began to lay the basis for a genuine Marxist alternative.

CHAPTER SEVEN

The Vietnamese Trotskyists: building an alternative to Stalinism

In the 1930s and then again at the end of World War II, revolutionary Marxists – Trotskyists – became a powerful force in the Vietnamese working class. As the French security police, the Sûreté, noted in February 1937: "The influence of the revolutionary agitators favourable to the Fourth International [followers of Trotsky] has grown in Cochin-China [South Vietnam], particularly in the working class milieux of Saigon-Cholon." In July 1937 it added: "The worker element has been won more by the Trotskyist party than by the PCI]."[57]

The founders of the Trotskyist movement in Vietnam were a small group of young Vietnamese students who had studied in France. The most prominent was Ta thu Thau, who had been involved in nationalist protests against colonial rule before going to study in France in 1927. Initially Thau was involved in the Annamite Independence Party (PAI) but as he moved to the left he made contact with the Trotskyist movement via the veteran revolutionary Alfred Rosmer. In 1929 in Paris Thau and a group of supporters organised a Trotskyist group, the Indochinese Left Opposition – they saw themselves as a left faction within the official Communist movement.

A key question that had propelled the young Vietnamese revolutionaries towards Trotskyism was the defeat of the 1925-27 Chinese revolution. The Stalinist Comintern argued that China was not ripe for socialist revolution but only for a nationalist revolution, and ordered the Chinese Communists to subordinate themselves to the bourgeois nationalist party, the Guomindang. This made it impossible for the Communists to lead the massive wave of worker and peasant revolt that was sweeping China to victory. The Communists' nationalist "allies", terrified by the revolutionary movement, unleashed a wave of terror against the working class and butchered the Communists. Stalin, in an attempt to give himself a left cover, then compounded the disaster by ordering the remaining Communists to launch a futile uprising which was savagely suppressed.

In response to the Stalinist line of subordinating the interests of workers and peasants of colonial countries to the national bourgeoisie, Ta thu Thau argued in 1930: "Only revolution based on the organisation of the proletariat and peasant masses is capable of liberating the colonies." He embraced Trotsky's theory of permanent revolution in opposition to Stalin's two stage theory of "bourgeois-democratic revolution" followed by a socialist revolution sometime in the distant future declaring:

> The question of independence must be merged with that of the proletarian revolution. The choice, "independence or slavery", now poses itself in another more concrete form: "socialism or nationalism".[58]

In 1930 Vietnamese students organised protests in France against the execution of the leaders of a nationalist uprising at Yen Bay. The authorities responded with a wave of arrests. Nineteen Vietnamese students, including Thau and his fellow Trotskyists Huynh van Phuong and Phan van Chanh, were forcibly repatriated to Saigon. They were to form the nucleus of the Trotskyist movement in Vietnam.

Under orders from Moscow the Stalinist Indochinese Communist Party (ICP), headed by Ho Chi Minh, launched armed uprisings in the countryside in 1930-1931. The revolts were brutally put down, with at least 10,000 Vietnamese massacred and 50,000 imprisoned. The crushing of this premature rebellion provoked a crisis amongst the surviving ICP cadres. Some of them became open to the arguments of the Trotskyists who sheeted home the blame to Stalin's sectarian ultraleft "Third Period" policy, which had been imposed on the Communist movement in the late 1920s and had led to a series of crushing defeats – most notably in Germany where it divided the working class and allowed Hitler to come to power.

One ICP activist, Dao hung Long, formed a breakaway group, the Communist League, which condemned the ICP leadership for its ultraleft adventurist policies and its failure to build seriously among workers. By May 1931 Long had been convinced of Trotskyism by Ho huu Tuong and they formed the International Communist League – usually called the October Group after the name of its paper. Ho huu Tuong had returned to Saigon in January 1931 after studying in France. Tuong, who had escaped the police repression after the student protests in Paris, had subsequently been won to Trotskyism. He became active in the Indochinese group of the Trotskyist French Communist League which by February 1932 had grown to about 40 students and published its own roneoed bulletin.

In November 1931 the various Trotskyist currents in Saigon united in the Indochinese Left Opposition, led by Ta thu Thau, Phan van Chanh, Dao hung Long and Ho huu Tuong. Operating underground, they produced a duplicated theoretical journal, a bimonthly agitational paper, *The Proletarian,* and translated basic Marxist writings such as the *Communist Manifesto* and Engels' *Socialism: Utopian and Scientific* into Vietnamese.

At its first conference in April 1932, differences arose as to whether they should attempt to operate as a left faction within the ICP or build a separate organisation, and over the question of clandestine work.[59] This led to a split and Thau formed the Indochinese Communism group. But "their movement, barely created, was temporarily broken up by repression". Sixty-five members and sympathisers were arrested in August 1932 and further arrests soon followed. In prison they were repeatedly tortured. One comrade, "Nguyen van Hoang ...unable to withstand his torture, hanged himself in his cell, and was cut down alive and kept naked in irons for more than two months."[60]

Thau was freed in January 1933 and quickly became involved in organising worker candidates for the Saigon municipal elections of April-May 1933. In a unique phenomenon for this period anywhere in the world, this "workers' panel" was a united front of Trotskyists, Stalinists and revolutionary nationalists. Its platform consisted of working class demands, such as the right to strike, the eight-hour-day and universal suffrage. It became known as the Struggle Group after its paper *La Lutte*. Two of its candidates, one Stalinist and one Trotskyist sympathiser, were elected.

La Lutte dissolved after the elections but was revived in October 1934. Stalinists and Trotskyists agreed to prepare for the coming elections on the basis of a common fight against the colonial administration and its auxiliary, the moderate nationalists of the Constitutional Party. They would restrict themselves to a paper for the defence of workers and peasants without broaching the questions of Stalinism or Trotskyism. This was a problematic approach which indicated that the young Trotskyist movement did not have a clear appreciation of the thoroughly counter-revolutionary politics of the Stalinists. Their decision to abstain from open criticism of Stalinism meant that the Trotskyists' supporters were not being politically educated in the difference between genuine revolutionary Marxist politics and the Stalinists' politics of class collaboration. It was a mistake for which they were to pay with their lives.

La Lutte restarted as a weekly and quickly achieved a mass following. In May 1935 one Trotskyist, one Trotskyist sympathiser and two Stalinists were elected to the Municipal Council, winning four of the six Vietnamese seats.

After being released from prison, Lu sanh Hanh, a former member of the ICP's Saigon Committee, linked up with Ho huu Tuong to launch in July 1935 an underground Trotskyist group, the League of International Communists for the Construction of the Fourth International – essentially the reformed October Group. By this stage the Stalinist Comintern was moving sharply to the right. Fearful of the rise of Hitler's Germany, Stalin was desperate for an alliance with the right-wing governments of France and Britain.

The Stalinist ICP, following the line of the French CP, called for the defence of France. The "legal" Trotskyists of *La Lutte* maintained an enforced silence about this betrayal of workers' interests and of the movement for independence in line with the agreement made with the Stalinists when *La Lutte* was established. But the underground League of International Communists maintained an unrelenting, bitter polemic against the

Stalinists' betrayals and also criticised the Trotskyists of *La Lutte* for not being critical enough of Stalinism. By June 1936 when its core leadership was arrested and tortured "they had recruited militants in about 40 workplaces".[61] Ho huu Tuong cohered the remaining underground Trotskyists and in September 1936 began legally publishing the first Trotskyist weekly in French, *Le Militant*. They worked with their fellow Trotskyists of *La Lutte* around the strikes that broke out in November at the Arsenal and the naval base and in December on the tramways and railways but maintained their criticism of *La Lutte's* softness on Stalinism.

"From the end of October 1936 to the end of August 1937, Vietnam was shaken by an unprecedented wave of strikes without an equivalent in any other French colony."[62] "The massive strike wave in France had its counterpart in Vietnam, where workers won the largest gains ever under the colonial regime...the Trotskyists, riding the energy of the strike wave, won the Saigon municipal elections, and in 1939 won 80 per cent of the vote for the Cochin China Colonial Council, the high-water mark of their influence prior to the 1945 insurrection."[63]

"In the course of this movement, at first spontaneous and then organised, workers and coolies set up action committees and strike committees under Trotskyist rather than Stalinist influence."[64] The authorities responded with repression. But the arrest of Thau and other leaders of *La Lutte* in September-October 1936 "and the hunger strike... they undertook for 11 days...caused huge indignation...in the villages close to Saigon, the merchants and hackney cab drivers struck...in Saigon demonstrations were underway, and the popularity of *La Lutte* had never been so great."[65] The authorities were forced to retreat, releasing Thau and his comrades.

The co-operation between Stalinists and Trotskyists could not last forever, in spite of the fact that the Trotskyists continued to make concessions to the Stalinists. The crunch came over the question of the French Popular Front government – a coalition between openly capitalist parties and worker-based parties – which was backed by the Stalinists. After the arrest of their leaders, the Trotskyists who had become the dominant group in *La Lutte,* having won to their standpoint a number of left nationalist activists, began to be more open in their criticism of the Popular Front government, which refused to grant independence to Vietnam and attacked workers' rights. In May 1937 Ho Chi Minh, under instructions from Moscow, ordered the ICP to break the united front with the Trotskyists whom the Stalinists now slandered as "fascists" because they opposed the French colonial authorities.

But the Trotskyists grew rapidly, winning over young militant workers and attracting "sympathisers in about 40 enterprises: among the dockers and postal workers, in the Arsenal, on the railways and trams...in the Water and Electricity Company...in the Manufactured Rubber Company...the three large bus depots..."[66]

Their influence started to spread from their base around Saigon into the rural areas and to the north. In response the French stepped up repression and there was a wave of arrests of strikers and Trotskyist supporters. But this did not stem the movement. Then in late 1938 there was a brief period of liberalisation and the Trotskyists redoubled their activity, with both groups publishing daily papers. By 1939 *La Lutte*'s membership reached 3,000.[67] The high point of their support was registered in the 1939 elections for the Colonial Council, in which *La Lutte* "won over 80 per cent of the votes; the bourgeois parties shared the rest and less than one per cent went to the discredited Stalinists, whose Saigon organisation split."[68] The Stalinists had been badly hurt in working class circles by their craven support for the French authorities. Ho Chi Minh reacted to this setback by declaring in a report to the Comintern:

> No reconciliation or concession is possible in relation to the Trotskyists. They must by all means be unmasked as agents of fascism; they must be politically exterminated.[69]

With the outbreak of World War II repression sharply intensified and the Trotskyist organisations, which had united in 1939, were broken, with many of their activists imprisoned in the Poulo Condore concentration camp or in Madagascar. After the fall of France, Japan took control of Vietnam but allowed the pro-fascist French authorities to administer the colony. The Stalinists survived World War II more intact than the Trotskyists, in part because of their backing from Moscow; but also because, after the entry of Russia into an alliance with the US and Britain, Ho Chi Minh received support from the US intelligence forces and the right-wing Chinese government.

However, operating underground, Lu sanh Hanh had by August 1944 regrouped several dozen supporters of the October Group as the League of International Communists (LCI. This small propaganda group contained "five founders of the Vietnamese Trotskyist movement, each with at least 12 years' experience of revolutionary struggle, and several experienced cadre formerly from the Hanoi section".[70] It was to lay the basis for rapid growth amongst the working class once the political situation opened up at the end of the war. By August 1945 the LCI claimed 200 members.[71]

In March 1945, facing looming defeat, the Japanese put an end to the French administration. A massive social crisis and power vacuum engulfed Vietnam, accentuated by a terrible famine that killed at least one million people. This set the scene for the Saigon insurrection of August-September 1945. With the collapse of the imperial authorities, the Vietnamese people thought the hour of independence had struck.

The situation was on a knife edge because Chinese, British and French forces were on their way to restore French rule. The ICP, ever loyal to Stalin, who had accepted the Great Power carve-up of the world and the allocation of Vietnam to France, was not prepared to lead a fight for Vietnamese independence. The Trotskyists, although badly weakened by the war, soon re-emerged in the streets, directly expressing a powerful popular mood for immediate independence and armed resistance to colonial restoration.

When *La Lutte*'s paper restarted in Saigon in August 1945 its print run went above 15,000, a considerable figure for a city of just 250,000. New Trotskyist groups emerged in the north and in provincial areas. *La Lutte* published a daily paper in Hanoi, which had a circulation of 30,000 in late 1945.[72] Ta thu Thau, half-paralysed due to torture, had been released from the Poulo Condor concentration camp in October 1944. He quickly resumed political activity but was murdered by the Stalinists while returning south from Hanoi in September 1945. Other leaders of *La Lutte* were executed by a Stalinist firing squad at the end of October 1945.

Faced with the imminent threat of a return of the French, the Trotskyists called for mass demonstrations and the arming of the population. On 21 August 1945 hundreds of thousands demonstrated in Saigon. The LCI mobilised 30,000 workers in its contingent on the march. People's committees in which the Trotskyists played a leading role sprang up everywhere. *La Lutte* organised some 18,000 militants and sympathisers and formed its own armed groups. In the mining area of Hongay-Campha in the north, workers formed workers' councils – soviets – that took total control of the area until they were crushed by Stalinist military forces.

The Stalinist ICP, now reformed as the Viet Minh, seized local government in much of the country. On 2 September 1945 the Viet Minh, playing a deceptive and treacherous role, declared independence – but a week later welcomed the arrival of British troops. *La Lutte* still had illusions in the Stalinists and thought it was possible to have joint work with them. The LCI and the people's committees it headed were more forthright in opposing the Stalinist government's capitulation to the imperialist powers. However, even they still had illusions in Stalinism. The LCI were not fully clear on the thoroughly counter-revolutionary nature of the Stalinists' politics, and the extent to which they were prepared to unleash murderous terror against their opponents on the left. This softness on Stalinism flowed, in part, from the fact that most Trotskyists in the 1930s still considered Stalin's Russia to be some form of workers' state.

The Trotskyists' lack of political clarity led to a truly disastrous error on 14 September 1945, when the Stalinist-led police surrounded the LCI headquarters where delegates of the people's committees were meeting. Rather than fighting off the Stalinists, the Trotskyists, showing incredible political naivety, surrendered. As I. Milton Sacks writes, "It seems that these Trotskyists still considered that they were part of the same movement as the Stalinists … the Viet Minh, for its part, displayed no such tender concern for the 'true militants'".[73] The Trotskyists were to pay with their lives. According to the LCI's own account:

> We conducted ourselves as true revolutionary militants. We let ourselves be arrested without using violence against the police, even though we were more numerous and all well armed. They took our machine guns and automatic pistols. They sacked our office, breaking furniture, ripping our flags, stealing the typewriters and burning all our papers.[74]

On 23 September the Saigon population rose up and for days had the imperialist forces surrounded in the centre of the city. The workers' militia organised by the remaining LCI members took part in the uprising. It was not until early October that the French regained control of Saigon. During this period Stalinist hit squads were eliminating

Trotskyists wherever they could find them. Hundreds more were killed by British and French troops.

By the end of October the workers' movement had been broken, and by 1946 colonial rule had been re-established, in no small part due to the policies of the Viet Minh led by Ho Chi Minh. It would take another 30 years of bloody war against the imperial powers, which saw millions killed, before the Vietnamese people were to achieve independence. This tragedy could well have been avoided if the Trotskyists had been able to win the leadership of the workers' and peasants' movement from the Stalinists – which at key points they had seemed to be on the brink of achieving.

Drawing a clear line

The Vietnamese Trotskyists showed that a tiny propaganda circle of self-sacrificing and dedicated Marxists could win mass working class support, even in the face of rivalry from a much larger Stalinist party, when the political circumstances were right. Their uncompromising opposition to imperialism and commitment to workers' power allowed them in the late 1930s (and again partially in 1945) to outflank the Stalinists and win a substantial working class following.

Unfortunately, their lack of appreciation of the utterly counter-revolutionary role of Stalinism left them unprepared for the scale of repression the Stalinists unleashed to break the Trotskyist movement. This serves to underline the vital importance of political clarity and the necessity of Marxists maintaining a strict political separation between their own organisations and those of their rivals on the left. This remains an important lesson for today when Marxists are still often confronted by well meaning people with the question: why doesn't all the left get together, after all you are all striving for the same goal.

But as the experience of Vietnam starkly confirms, this was simply not the case. Indeed it was quite the reverse. The Stalinists and the Trotskyists were fighting for entirely different and counterposed goals. The Trotskyists were fighting to lead a working-class revolution which would defeat colonial rule and establish a new social order democratically controlled by the mass of workers, urban poor and peasants and to spread that revolution to other countries.

In contradistinction, the Stalinists had nothing but contempt for the masses. They wanted to ride to power on the back of the mass of workers and peasants and establish a brutal bureaucratic state, a state which they would control and gain enormous privileges from and which would in turn compete with other nation states on the world capitalist market. The collapse of Stalinism in Eastern Europe struck a decisive blow to Stalinist domination of the left internationally. Nonetheless there are still currents on the left that look uncritically to the regimes in Vietnam, China, North Korea or Cuba as some form of socialism or "workers' state". There is no way that Marxists whose touchstone is the self-emancipation of the working class can unite with organisations whose vision of "freedom" is these brutal dictatorships.

CHAPTER EIGHT

The last upturn: Case No 1 – the revolutionary left in Italy

The profound radicalisation of the late 1960s and early 1970s opened up the first serious opportunity in decades for the rebirth on a mass scale of the revolutionary left internationally. New revolutionary groups emerged or in some cases tiny pre-existing groups expanded rapidly. None of the revolutionary groups were ultimately successful in establishing parties that could seriously challenge the hold of the reformist or Stalinist Communist parties over the mass of workers. Nevertheless, in country after country groups of some thousands or tens of thousands did emerge and in some cases seemed for a few short years to be on the brink of a decisive breakthrough. So their experiences are instructive, both negatively and positively.

May '68 in France has gone down in history as the high point of revolutionary up-heaval in the 1960s but in many ways the Italian events of 1969-70 were more profound. The depth of the worker-student alliance was greater and the ferment in society more lasting. For while 1969-1970 was the high point of struggle, Italian capitalism was not really restabilised until 1976.[75] There were eight years of enormous social turmoil that challenged the organisation of Italian society at every level. In 1972 in a period of three months, 1200 schools, institutes and universities were occupied. Moreover, the Italian revolutionaries were far more influential than in France or pretty much anywhere else. According to Yurii Colombo, "between 1968 and the late 1970s more than 100,000 people became members of far-left organizations in Italy."[76]

In July 1969 the unions called a one-day general strike against rent rises. However, the workers at Turin's giant Mirafiori FIAT car plant – Italy's largest factory – were far from impressed. Throughout May and June they had waged a series of strikes co-ordinated by a worker/student assembly under revolutionary leadership. They planned their own action for the general strike. On the day several thousand workers set out from the gates of FIAT. The official union slogan was "no more rent rises". However, the demonstration from FIAT had a slogan all its own, destined to send a shiver down the collective spine of the ruling class – "What do we want? Everything!" The march soon clashed with police. The workers responded by constructing barricades and fighting running battles far into the night. In the aftermath there were mass assemblies in FIAT and other Turin factories, which involved thousands of workers and students debating out the issues.

The influence of revolutionary students at FIAT was not a fleeting episode. The struggle for a new contract in the metal industry some months later saw an explosion of militancy. The revolutionaries who had won a wide audience at FIAT succeeded in gaining support among young workers at dozens of factories. They led another week-long strike at FIAT in November 1969, then a 15-day struggle that brought production virtually to a halt in July 1970. Huge worker columns went from one part of the plant to another, breaking through the gates separating the assembly works from the body plant. Revolutionary students joined in one such demonstration which involved 10,000 workers, each with a spanner in their hands, chanting "Agnelli, Indochina is in your factory."[77] This was the Italian long hot autumn.

The beginnings

The Italian economic miracle of the 1950s and 1960s saw the highest growth rates in Europe. Italy was transformed from a predominantly rural society into an industrial powerhouse. Millions of workers were drawn into the giant factories of northern Italy from the poverty-stricken south. But modernisation concealed enormous social tensions. Southern migrant workers were housed in horrid conditions in northern cities and faced speed up, unsafe conditions and authoritarian managers. As early as 1962 this pressure cooker atmosphere led to an explosion of rioting in Turin. But it was students who first moved into generalised revolt. Italian universities expanded rapidly and chaotically. Entry exams and quotas were abolished in 1965 and student numbers skyrocketed, without an increase in facilities. Rome University, designed for 5,000 students, had 60,000. Student grievances proliferated. But what brought them to a sharp focus was the Gui bill that sought to restrict university entry. In 1967 opposition to the government turned into a 55-day occupation of the Milan Polytechnic architecture faculty and an occupation at Pisa that led to clashes with police.[78]

The initial issues of fees, course content and exams generalised to broader issues as a wave of occupations engulfed the campuses and spread to the high schools. In January 1968 thirty-six universities were occupied. It was a revolt against all the old values – against the family and for sexual liberation, against individualism and consumerism. A key turning point came at Rome University in March 1968, where in the battle of Valle Giulia occupying students, after being evicted by police, fought to recapture the university. After a police baton charge, students set cars and vans alight. Forty-six police were hospitalised. "It was the first time we hadn't retreated in front of the police, the first time we took the initiative and advanced on them."[79] It marked a sharp change from protest to overt resistance. The movement was chaotic, spontaneist, largely middle class with many utopian aspects, but to its credit, it rapidly began to look to the working class. One historian wrote:

> The Italian students were not so Utopian as to believe that they were going to change the world by themselves. Unlike the bulk of the German student movement, which dismissed the working class as irredeemably integrated, and unlike Marcuse, who put the emphasis on marginal groups as the true revolutionaries, the Italian students never thought for a moment that they were the revolutionary class... The student movement of 1968, therefore turned rapidly... towards the factories. It was there, they argued, that the decisive battles were to be fought.[80]

This is an exaggeration. There were groups that glorified student power. But it is true that Marxist ideas – in the broadest sense – rapidly became hegemonic in the student movement. In part this reflected a long tradition of pro-working class politics amongst the left on the state universities.[81] But even at the elite Catholic universities a movement originally motivated by radical Catholicism began to read Marx and turn to the working class. The Italian Communist Party (PCI) was, however, beyond the pale for many of the newly radicalised students. It was rightly seen as an integrated opposition – loyal to capitalism. For the first time since World War II a radical movement had erupted outside the control of the PCI and threatened its long domination of the left.

How are we to explain this bypassing of the traditional party of Italian radicalism, which in the 1960s claimed 1.5 million members? It reflected both the depth of the radicalisation and the contradictory nature of student life. Because students in those years were largely drawn from the middle class, they did not have a strong tradition of support for the PCI – unlike the workers of northern and central Italy.[82] Having rebelled against their parents' conservative values, they had no time for half-measures. They sought a totally revolutionary alternative. Furthermore, on campus students did not have to deal with the traditional working class organisations – the unions in particular – which provided the reformist parties with a stable implantation. This, combined with other factors – the depth of the intellectual ferment, the youth of the students and so on – meant they were capable of being rapidly radicalised in large numbers. But given the students' lack of social power this radicalism could equally rapidly dissipate unless they quickly established a base within a section of the only class with the power to transform capitalism.

Unfortunately the tiny pre-existing revolutionary groups were politically confused or sectarian and were overwhelmed by the upsurge. That meant that the tens of thousands of students who turned in a Marxist direction virtually had to start from scratch to create their own revolutionary groups – and in the process they embraced a confused welter of ideas. If in the mid-60s even a small Marxist group had existed with a clear critique of Stalinism, a rejection of ultraleftism, a tradition of open debate and an orientation towards intervening in the political arguments taking place, it could have had a decisive positive impact on the movement. For while the politics of traditional Stalinism – the PCI – were discredited in the radical student milieu, Stalinist *ideas* were far from dead. Seemingly radical Stalinist politics – Maoism, Che Guevara-style guerrilla struggle and Ho Chi Minh's Vietnamese Communist Party – had widespread appeal. Even some socialist currents that claimed to reject Stalinism were influenced by these supposedly more "revolutionary" Stalinist ideas. This failure to break decisively with Stalinism led to devastating demoralisation later in the seventies, as China's rapprochement with the US and the horrors of Pol Pot's Kampuchea exposed the true nature of Maoism.

The turn to the working class by the student revolutionaries proved extraordinarily successful because of the ferment welling up from below. Without that all the energy and commitment of the students would have come to naught. Marxist groups can't recruit large numbers of workers by an act of will. Two things are required to establish a substantial working-class base: firstly a critical mass of revolutionaries (students, ex-students and young workers) – not tens but some hundreds or thousands; secondly a generalised ferment within the working class – not just a wave of strikes, but a broad social rebellion. Without these preconditions any attempt to "go to the working class" can easily break the neck of the revolutionaries.

Why is this the case? Workers, particularly older workers with family commitments and so on, are less likely than students to join a small socialist group which is incapable of leading struggles to improve their living standards. They want a party with a real base that can lead major struggles and deliver real gains. It is only when the revolutionaries become large enough to offer a practical alternative to the reformist parties and union leaders in day-to-day struggles that they can recruit workers in large numbers. Whereas on campus, small socialist groups can in the right circumstances have an impact disproportionate to their numbers. This means that a revolutionary group can grow significantly out of student movements even before there is a generalised radicalisation in society.

To build on firm foundations what is needed above all is a sober analysis which rigorously assesses the possibilities of the movement so they can make the most of the opportunities that open up. However, a tradition of such debate is not established overnight. It has to be fought for over a period of years. This was something the Italian far left discovered to their cost. Because of the theoretical confusion of the movement, in part inevitable given its newness, any serious discussion of strategy was ignored. Indeed attempts to even *discuss* strategy tended to be dismissed or at times even condemned as a form of betrayal. It was seen as an admission of the possibility of defeat. Voluntarism reigned supreme as the movement plunged forward. While it was riding the tide of radicalisation, this was no disaster – but terrible shocks were in store when the movement suffered setbacks in the mid 1970s.

The politics of the far left and the lessons for today

The revolutionaries could gain a hearing because by the late 1960s a significant gap had opened up between the union leadership (often CPers) and the mass of workers. Indeed, in many workplaces shopfloor union organisation was weak. It was into this space that the revolutionaries inserted themselves. Students went to the factory gates to link up with workers – they handed out leaflets and joined picket lines. They brought the methods of the student movement, particularly their mass assemblies, to the young workers. At FIAT in Turin it was the mass assemblies of thousands of young workers and the so-called "externals" – the student revolutionaries – that led some of the great struggles of the period. They gave birth to the largest revolutionary group, Lotta Continua, whose weekly paper had a print run of 65,000 copies by November 1969. It soon became a daily, and Lotta Continua's membership quickly reached the 10,000 mark.[83]

Lotta Continua's origins were in a group of intellectuals which included Toni Negri and Mario Tronti, known as "workerists", around the journal *Quaderni Rossi*. This group gained influence in the Pisa area in 1967. "This was not just workerist and spontaneist. It also contained a strong dose of Maoism."[84] The group split when one faction argued for a national organisation with a defined leadership. The leader of the other faction, Adriano Sofri, argued for a more "spontaneist" approach. Sofri and his supporters went to Turin to get involved in the struggles at FIAT and soon dominated both the worker-student assemblies and Lotta Continua. Lotta Continua denounced the unions as "bourgeois" and opposed having union delegates in the workplaces. It called instead for all decisions to be made by mass assemblies:

> Either the political and mass organisation of the workers, guided by a revolutionary vanguard with its own means of co-ordination, actively working against the union. Or union organisation. That is the choice that we must make.[85]

In the most militant workplaces at the high point of struggle, Lotta Continua's slogan "we are all delegates" had a resonance. But ultimately it was self-defeating. It isolated militants from those who still had some confidence in the unions. By abstaining from standing for positions of delegates it made it easier for the union leaders to re-establish a base on the shop floor. Far from them being swept aside, the unions grew rapidly. By 1975 the two main union federations organised 46.2 per cent of the workforce compared with 31 per cent in 1967.[86]

In the other key northern city of Milan, the lead was given by the giant Pirelli tyre factory. Pirelli workers had been disillusioned when, after a three-day strike in early 1968, union officials accepted very modest pay increases. As a result, a group of experienced worker militants, together with student radicals – some of whom were to form the core of the revolutionary group Avanguardia Operia (AO) – organised a united base committee (CUB) to carry on the struggle. The unions and the PCI were denounced for their compromises and after many months of fierce struggle the workers won significant gains. This became the model for other base committees in Milan.

AO, in part, had its origins as a semi-Maoist split from the small Orthodox Trotskyist Gruppi Comunisti Rivoluzionari. AO saw itself as Leninist and anti-Stalinist. Yet it embraced the Chinese Cultural Revolution. It criticised Lotta Continua as "spontaneist" and the other main far left group Il Manifesto for "centrism".[87] AO was not as ultraleft on the question of how to relate to reformist organisations as Lotta Continua, arguing that "they still had much room for manoeuvre".[88] AO built more slowly and methodically at first. By the early 1970s it had 3,000 militants in Milan. It then expanded at great speed by fusing with a variety of groups in other cities.[89] Its leadership were sophisticated revolutionaries, but in 1969-70 they posed the rank-and-file CUB groups as an alternative to the unions and, like Lotta Continua, rejected work within the newly formed factory councils.

A profound change was coming over the student movement. It was losing its libertarian and spontaneous character – the emphasis began to be on organisation and the need to lay the basis for a revolutionary party which would wrest workers' loyalties from the PCI. The students had learnt the lesson of the French May, where enormous revolutionary possibilities were let slip due to the lack of revolutionary leadership. They were determined not to let the opportunity slip in Italy. This is an important point. All over the world May 68 had a decisive impact. It was not simply that it showed that workers and students could rise up and challenge capitalism; though that was vital in inspiring a new generation of revolutionaries. However, socialist groups didn't grow by basking in the reflected glory of Paris. They had to win an ideological argument about the role of the Communist parties and reformist politics more generally – that working within the official channels of the system leads you to sabotage revolutionary upheavals. And that this in turn made it vital to build a revolutionary party. Revolutionaries in Italy, Britain and Australia did not grow because there was some campaign to intervene in support of May '68 but because they made a political argument about the need to build in their own country.

All of the three main revolutionary organisations in Italy grew in the years 1969-72, absorbing many of those who in 1968 had been unorganised spontaneists. They became a significant force within the most active sections of the working class. Indeed by 1973 the far left had tens of thousands of organised followers, three daily papers and a number of radio stations. In Milan in the mid-1970s the far left could regularly mobilise 20,000-30,000 on the streets and had a strong presence in the high schools. However, as the struggle began to recede, many young people and workers who had been radicalised in the previous few years began to look with hope to the PCI, to the prospect of changing things through an election victory. The PCI was aided by a series of weaknesses in the politics of the far left – above all the idea that the influence of reformism would be spontaneously swept away by mass struggle. Nevertheless it was to take another six years for the union leaders and the PCI to totally regain their control over the insurgent movement.

The ebbing of social struggles after 1974 threw the far left into a deep crisis. Lotta Continua flipped over from its ultraleft stance and adopted a much less critical approach to the PCI. In 1975 its main slogan became "The Communist Party to the government".[90] On the other hand, a minority of the far left turned to terrorism, which took on a broader form in Italy than in any other European country, and which further contributed to the disorientation of the working class. As Tim Potter observed:

> ... all the groups of the revolutionary left entered a deep crisis from which they were not to recover. Thousands of militants had been brought up in the belief that the socialist revolution was at hand...Their dreams had been brutally dashed and...a significant number were to drift towards the terrorist embrace. In the factories there was a layer of militants who had fought for almost a decade against the bosses and their own union leadership. The struggle now appeared lost, and some drifted towards the "armed party". Added to this was a vast pool of young people, often unemployed, wanting to change Italian society but seeing no channel other than the armed groups.[91]

Much of the remainder of the far left moved to the right and downplayed the radical, activist forms of struggle. In 1976, the three leading far left organisations stood jointly in the elections under the banner Democrazia Proletaria but their vote was extremely disappointing. In the end the revolutionary opportunities were squandered. Because of the weaknesses of the politics of the young revolutionaries, in particular the continuing legacy of Stalinism, the groups that emerged in the late 1960s were not able to survive the downturn of struggle in the late 1970s. But, and this is the *key* point, they had for all their weaknesses shown what was possible. With the collapse of Stalinism, the opportunities next time round will be even greater. The lessons of the experience of the Italian far left in the 1960s and 1970s are vital if we are to seize the moment when our turn comes.

It can be tempting to think that if socialists can just hang on until the next radical upsurge, it will solve all our problems. But growth is not inevitable or automatic, even when the political climate changes dramatically. Revolutionaries have to be able to intervene – to make political arguments that convince people – otherwise they can simply be bypassed by struggles. With the collapse of the Stalinist Communist parties, and with the ALP so discredited, it may seem that when an upsurge comes Marxists will face no credible reformist competitors and so it will be all smooth sailing. But when the political climate shifts decisively to the left, the existing reformists – the ALP left, sections of the union leadership, the Greens or whoever – will repackage themselves to appear more radical and will grow rapidly or alternatively new radical sounding reformist organisations will emerge like Syriza in Greece or Podemos in Spain. In those circumstances, unless revolutionaries know how to relate to workers influenced by reformist ideas and understand the role of union leaders, they will be profoundly disoriented and marginalised.

That's why what socialists do in the here and now – the sometimes humdrum routine of building an organisation – matters. At the most obvious level the bigger a socialist organisation is, the better placed it will be to make gains when the level of struggle rises and the political climate shifts sharply. But just as importantly, the experience and political education socialists gain from building an organisation today, the ability to make arguments, to democratically debate out a way forward, to understand what is wrong with reformist politics, studying how socialists in the past dealt with these problems, learning about the traditions of the socialist movement – all are vital preparation. Theoretical education combined with the practical experience of intervening with political arguments in the debates and struggles of today and attempting to play a leading role in building the various small campaigns that arise in the here and now is key to training a larger layer of socialists – a cadre – capable of leading their fellow workers and students in the major struggles of the future.

CHAPTER NINE

The last upturn: Case No 2 – the International Socialists in Britain

The radical upsurge of the 1960s was not as profound in Britain as in Italy; nonetheless it opened up important opportunities for revolutionaries to break out of the long years of extreme isolation imposed upon them by a combination of the post-war boom and the Stalinist domination of the left. The most successful of the small revolutionary groups was the International Socialists (IS), later the Socialist Workers Party (SWP), which was to become the leading organisation in the International Socialist Tendency (IST). The IS, which started from just a few hundred members in the mid 1960s, was able to seize the opportunity of the campus rebellion of the late 1960s to recruit significant numbers of radical students who in turn were able to carry out a successful turn to the working class during the industrial upsurge of the early seventies.[92]

There was a rising wave of industrial struggle from 1969 through to 1974. The number of strike days rose from 4.7 million in 1968 to 13.6 million in 1971 to 23.9 million in 1972.[93] Major struggles included the 1971 Clyde work-in, the 1972 national miners' strike and a wave of factory occupations. The climax came in the winter of 1973-74 with the miners' struggle which brought down Ted Heath's Tory government. The IS went from having 447 members at the beginning of 1968 to 4,000 at the high point of the struggle against Heath.

The origins of the IS lay in the Trotskyist movement – the revolutionary opposition to the Stalinist Communist parties. In the late 1930s the Trotskyists had predicted that World War II would bring a profound economic crisis, the collapse of Stalinism in Russia and an escalating wave of revolt. It did not pan out that way. Stalinism came out of the war strengthened, not weakened. There *were* mass upheavals at the end of the war but they were derailed by the Communist parties and reformist Labor parties. As the Trotskyists falteringly tried to face up to this painful reality, the movement disintegrated. The key issue was the Russian question. The mainstream of the Trotskyist movement – the "orthodox Trotskyists" – continued to argue that Russia was a degenerated workers' state. They declared that the regimes imposed on Eastern Europe by Russian tanks were "deformed" workers' states. This represented an abandonment of the basic Marxist standpoint that "the emancipation of the working class is the task of the working class itself".

A small minority of the British Trotskyist group, the Revolutionary Communist Party (RCP), led by the Palestinian-born Marxist Tony Cliff, rejected the idea that Stalinist Russia or its Eastern European satellites had anything to do with socialism. Instead they argued that the Stalinist regimes were state capitalist societies in which workers were exploited by a bureaucratic ruling class. They adopted the slogan "Neither Washington nor Moscow, but International Socialism".[94]

In June 1949 the badly disoriented RCP was formally dissolved into a clandestine body called "the Club" headed by Gerry Healy. Soon afterwards the comrades who held the "state capitalist" position were either expelled or left, and in 1950 began to publish a duplicated journal, *Socialist Review*.[95] The Socialist Review Group (SRG) was tiny with 21 people at its first conference and a claimed membership of 33.[96] A mere 350 copies of the first issue of their journal were produced.

The other key issue the SRG had to come to grips with was the post-war boom. The perspective the movement inherited from Trotsky was one of growing crisis leading to massive revolutionary possibilities. But the first duty of revolutionaries is to look reality in the face, and in the early 1950s Western capitalism was palpably not collapsing. In the course of the 1950s the SRG was to put forward the Permanent Arms Economy theory to explain the nature and limitations of the post-war boom.[97] This enabled the SRG/IS to acknowledge the reality of the boom and to avoid the catastrophist fantasies of some orthodox Trotskyists. "At the same time, however", as Alex Callinicos point out "the theory predicted that capitalism was experiencing an only temporary stabilization." This helped them to avoid the adaptation to reformism that characterised various Trotskyist currents.[98]

As one historian of the movement, Ian Birchall, writes:

> Splits are not to be undertaken lightly in the revolutionary movement. Unity of action combined with full and fraternal debate is often a preferable solution. But when the whole question of political direction and strategy is at stake, a split becomes inevitable. In these terms the split of 1950 was justified.[99]

A tiny, fragile group like the SRG could have easily collapsed or retreated from trying to build and become a mere talk shop that gradually faded away. This is what has happened to innumerable small bands of socialists, even in times a lot more favourable than the 1950s – the harshest decade of the twentieth century for revolutionaries in the Western capitalist countries. For a small revolutionary group to go forward "everything depends", as Alex Callinicos put it, on the existence of a hard core of individuals rooted in the revolutionary tradition and having the determination, energy, capacity and commitment to build an organisation, however long it takes and however tough the situation. Where this core exists, there is a reasonable chance of success. Where it does not – and there is no simple or artificial way of creating it – then, however promising the context, the group will not flourish.[100]

It was a real struggle to survive the fifties. In 1958 the group nearly folded when a majority of members, with only three opposed – Cliff, Jean Tait and Chanie Rosenberg – voted to dissolve the SRG into the ultra-sectarian Socialist Labour League (SLL. The proposal fell through but it reveals what pressure they were under. Throughout the fifties the SRG was purely a propaganda group; it was not able to make any meaningful intervention in the class struggle. The propaganda they were putting forward in their paper was very general propaganda about the big issues in society – the nature of Stalinism, the Permanent Arms Economy, and the nature of reformism. As Tony Cliff explained,

> We were not even operating at the level of concrete propaganda. All this was abstract propaganda. There is no alternative when you are speaking to a few dozen people.[101]

But as Birchall writes:

> Marxists are not fatalists, and in any historical period there is something for a revolutionary to do. But there are historical situations where objective factors prevent revolutionary ideas from reaching a mass audience. In such a situation small groups can play a vital role simply in keeping the revolutionary flame alive. Marx in a letter to Bolte wrote: "Sects are justified (historically) as long as the working class is not yet ripe for an independent historical movement.

> But to accept the necessity for a sect is not to justify sectarianism. A correct analysis on its own guarantees nothing. A number of other groupings with a state capitalist analysis of Russia emerged around this time in various parts of the world. Most of them either just disappeared, or got lost in the lunatic fringe of sectarian politics...

> A propaganda group has to have an audience; and unless a revolutionary group remains in intimate contact with its audience, the dangers of falling into a complete fantasy world are great indeed.[102]

In practice this meant work in the Labour Party. As Cliff put it: "It was necessary to have regular political discussion with people outside the group, and the only place you could do so at that time was the Labour Party."[103] "The Labour Party was seen as an arena which made it possible to keep contact with the working class movement, and as a source of recruits."[104] The main focus, however, was not on the adult party but on the Labour League of Youth. Nevertheless, we are talking about recruiting individuals here and there, not sizeable numbers.

The small size of the SRG – it still only had 60 members in 1960 – prevented it benefiting significantly from the dramatic events of 1956 – most importantly the Hungarian workers' revolution against Stalinism – that led to a sharp rupture in the

British Communist party which lost 10,000 members. The SRG was overshadowed by the somewhat larger, but sectarian SLL, which recruited considerable numbers of CP activists, only to chew them up and spit them out over the following couple of years. However, according to Cliff, although the SRG "did not expand very much as a result of the Hungarian Revolution...qualitatively it was significant. We became harder and more convinced in the rightness of our position (on the nature of Stalinism)."[105]

In the early 1960s new possibilities opened up with the emergence of the Campaign for Nuclear Disarmament (CND) which organised marches of 100,000 at Easter 1960 and 1961. CND radicalised a generation of young people. The SRG focused on the Labour Party youth group, the Young Socialists (YS), which attracted many of those radicalised by CND. The newly formed YS quickly grew to something like 40,000 members many of whom were young workers.

Inside the YS there were lively debates over the Russian question, in particular over the "workers' bomb" – that is whether socialists should oppose nuclear weapons in Russia as well as in the West. The SRG, which was involved with the radical youth paper *Young Guard*, opposed nuclear weapons both East and West. This approach sharply differentiated it from the Communist Party and some orthodox Trotskyist groups that backed the Russian bomb. This stance undoubtedly helped the SRG, which changed its name to International Socialism (IS) in 1962, to recruit. Most young workers unsurprisingly did not fancy being obliterated by Russian nukes. Birchall describes the typical political evolution of a young comrade at this time:

> first get involved in CND demonstrations, then join the Young Socialists, and, via *Young Guard*, come into IS ...Recruits were being made on the basis of ideas rather than activity – indeed, IS did not have activity of its own, as distinct from participating in the activities of the Young Socialists and CND.[106]

Prior to its intervention in the YS membership grew very slowly from 33 in 1950 to 60 in 1960. But

> by 1964 our membership was 200, a modest but good success. The experience ... in the YS produced a qualitative advance. Even more important, the new recruits played a leading role in what was a mass movement. They learned how to intervene in a mass movement.[107]

One of the key ingredients of their success

> was a sense of proportion, of the relative insignificance of IS as an organisation. When IS had two hundred members...the question at stake was not the "crisis of leadership"...It was the much more modest task of educating those who were around to listen and of striking roots in the class in a small way where this was possible.[108]

> New comrades were involved in activity, participated in meetings and – somewhat unsystematically – were introduced to the group's political positions. This was important in that the comrades, while being aware that they were in a tiny minority, felt themselves

part of a broader movement – CND or Labour Party left – and thus never had the sense of isolation from reality so easily generated by sectarian politics.[109]

The IS maintained a strong orientation to the working class and in the early 1960s published *Labour Worker*, which was intended to be more agitational and geared to relating to industrial struggle. Workers were recruited but as individuals on the basis of the general politics of revolutionary socialism rather than as an industrial strategy for intervening in the broader class struggle.

When a socialist group is small it needs to put very serious effort into following up and talking to contacts. You need to take every individual contact seriously. This is the bread and butter of building. It is part of what Trotsky called the primitive accumulation of cadres. So for a period in the sixties, the IS's main leader Tony Cliff every week went to the ENV factory in London, where the IS had one member, to talk to some shop stewards. Eventually from this steady, detailed work the IS established a factory branch of 12 at ENV.

When Labour was elected in 1964 all the steam went out of the left opposition in the party and the potential for recruitment in the YS dried up. Over the next few years, as disillusionment with Labour grew, the IS gradually and rather unsystematically dropped out of the Labour Party. Instead the IS concentrated on strike support work, selling a book they produced opposing Labour's Incomes Policy, and got heavily involved in tenants' struggles. By the end of 1967 IS membership had increased slowly but significantly to over 400, compared to 200-odd when Labour came to office.

The sixties upsurge

Then in 1968 revolutionaries suddenly found themselves swimming with the stream. As in virtually every other Western country May '68 in Paris had a marked impact. A *New Society* survey taken on the October 1968 Vietnam demonstration showed that 68 per cent of those marching were not just against the war, but against capitalism in general. In March 1967 the London School of Economics (LSE saw one of the first of the international wave of student occupations. Student militancy then spread right across the campuses. The first sizeable Vietnam demonstration occurred in October 1967 with 15,000-20,000 marching. In March 1968 an even larger demonstration attempted to storm the US embassy, and then in October 1968 100,000 marched.

Yet in the mid-sixties the number of socialists active on campus was minuscule, and they had virtually no influence over the mass of students. Only a dozen people attended the LSE Socialist Society's founding meeting in 1965. Before the March 1967 LSE occupation "IS students had played little systematic part in student politics, and certainly had no thought-out strategy for student work."[110] In February 1967 there were perhaps six IS members active in the LSE, but by May 1968 there were about 30. Cliff relates that

"At the time (of the occupation) I spent a month in the London School of Economics arguing and we recruited something like 40 members."[111]

IS activists played a key role in many of the student struggles of 1967-69, leading half the occupations, and attracted around them many of the most militant students. But the IS recruited students – and this was stressed continuously – on the basis of an orientation to workers. An IS leaflet distributed at the March 1968 anti-Vietnam demo argued for a decisive turn to the working class: "A blow against the boss is a blow against the Vietnam war."[112] The IS sold 10,000 copies of a book by Cliff on incomes policy and shop stewards and picked up a few militant workers. It then initiated rank and file groups in the unions, firstly among teachers. The IS approach was based on an insightful analysis of the class struggle in the boom years. They argued that full employment had led to "a shift in the locus of reformism".[113] Workers were able

> to achieve significant improvements in their standard of living through small-scale wage disputes ... Consequently, the social-democratic and Communist parties, oriented on parliamentary reform, became less important to rank-and-file workers. The latter's most intense loyalties were attached instead to informal workplace institutions such as ... shop stewards, directly responsive to trade unionists' pressures and effective instruments of the guerrilla warfare in the factories ...The political apathy of the "affluent worker" ... lamented by many ... commentators ... represented not the end of the class struggle but its diversion into different channels. The increasing difficulties experienced by the world economy in the second half of the 1960s, however, meant that the ruling class would be compelled to curtail this "do-it-yourself reformism"...The resulting confrontation between capitalist offensive and a militant, self-confident rank and file would be explosive, particularly because of the decay of the mass reformist organisations.[114]

The IS probably gained more from the movement of 1968 than all the other left groups in Britain put together. They were aided by the extreme sectarianism of their major orthodox Trotskyist rival, the SLL, which condemned the movement against the Vietnam war as petty bourgeois protest politics. At the biggest anti-war demo the SLL handed out a leaflet headed: "Why the Socialist Labour League is not marching". The IS began 1968 as a scattering of local groups with 447 members and a monthly paper; by the end of the year they were a national organisation of a thousand members, with a weekly paper, *Socialist Worker*, selling 7,000 copies, many to industrial workers.

> This transformation did not take place smoothly. Many of the most enthusiastic new members did not fully understand the basic tenets of revolutionary Marxism. So intense was the debate at the organisation's autumn conference that there had to be a repeat conference two months later. But it was worthwhile. In spring and summer 1969 a decisive transformation took place in the class struggle in Britain, and the International Socialists were in a much better position to intervene in this than they had been a year earlier.[115]

"By the middle of 1969 the wave of revolutionary euphoria had subsided, and it was much clearer that the struggle ahead was to be a protracted one."[116] IS membership hovered around the thousand mark until early in 1971; some workers joined and so did students from the occupations of 1970, but some recruits from 1968 dropped out as their exaggerated revolutionary expectations wilted. However, in 1971 the IS began to grow quickly again, in part because the movement suffered setbacks that led some activists to look for political answers. The IS recruited from intervention in industrial disputes, and out of campaigns against racism and against the British occupation of Northern Ireland. The print run of *Socialist Worker* rose to 27,000 in February 1972. The IS initiated rank-and-file papers aimed at workers in specific industries. By September 1973 forty or so factory or industrial branches had been set up. At the high point of the mass struggle against the Heath government in 1974, *Socialist Worker*'s print run rose from 30,000 to over 50,000 with a paid sale of around 35,000.[117] Membership reached 4,000. Not that they got everything right. As Cliff later acknowledged:

> The turn to the working class in the late 1960s and early 1970s led to serious distortions in our activities. It encouraged the wholesale abandonment of student work, justified by "workerism", which was especially rampant among ex-students.[118]

The election of the Labour government in 1974 proved a decisive turning point in the class struggle. Initially the IS thought Labour would have a brief honeymoon of a few months, after which massive struggles would erupt. Things did not work out that way. The Labour government managed to roll back many working class gains by co-opting union leaders to police the workers' movement via a social contract that held down wages. This ushered in a long downturn in struggle which made it much harder going for the revolutionary left.

The difficulties of adjustment to this less favourable climate led to growing tensions in IS – renamed the Socialist Workers Party (SWP) in 1977. It suffered a split that took out about 150 members, including experienced leading figures. It "went through an acute crisis at the end of the 1970s, in which the main issues were, first the very question of whether or not the upturn which had brought down Heath was over, and second, the problem of how to relate the 'new social movements' responding to various forms of oppression (of women, blacks, gays, etc.) to the working-class struggle for socialism."[119] But unlike in Italy, the downturn did not lead to the disintegration of the revolutionary left. By 1980 SWP membership had recovered to 4100. As Chris Harman summed up:

> The party's ability to survive was a product of its politics. In 1968 and afterwards, the influence of the International Socialists prevented the new revolutionary socialists in Britain being captivated by the Maoist and Guevarist ideas that were so powerful in many other countries. That turn avoided the political disillusionment with China and Kampuchea which elsewhere combined with the demoralisation of temporary defeat to produce a flight from politics. In "this most bourgeois of bourgeois countries", where parliamentarianism has traditionally dominated, the revolutionary left continues to exist, albeit on the margins of the working-class movement.[120]

CHAPTER TEN

Is there an easier road?

The argument that small groups of socialists need to start by first building a socialist propaganda group if they are to have any hope of laying secure foundations for a mass revolutionary party is by no means widely accepted by socialists today.[121] Socialist Alternative's approach has been condemned by some sections of the left as narrow, rigid and sectarian or is dismissed as at best utopian. For some this is because they reject outright the need for a distinctively revolutionary party. A diminishing band of socialists still hold to the idea of trying to influence the ALP.[122] Some look to parties like the Greens. In the US some socialists, including the right wing of the Democratic Socialists of America (DSA), aim to reform or push to the left the bourgeois Democratic Party. Others on the left argue that a "broad" socialist party which includes revolutionaries and reformists and all shades in between can substitute for a revolutionary party.

It is not simply the worst elements of the soft left and cynical former revolutionaries who promote the view that building a propaganda group with distinctive revolutionary politics is sectarian and counter-productive. Variants of these views are put forward by a number of organised socialist groups in Australia and internationally. For a period the examples of Syriza in Greece and Podemos in Spain were widely promoted as the alternative road forward for socialists.[123]

Murray Smith, formerly of the Scottish Socialist Party (SSP) and the French Revolutionary Communist League (LCR), was for many years one of the strongest advocates of the broad party model.[124] Initially Smith pointed to the examples of the SSP and Communist Refoundation in Italy – "the phenomenon of the appearance of new parties or alliances that do not fit into the classic reformist or revolutionary categories and that have a capacity to develop". "The mass revolutionary parties of the future... will be open, pluralist and non-hierarchical."[125]

Subsequently he championed the Tsipras leadership of Syriza in Greece, the very leadership that went on to impose even harsher austerity measures on the Greek working class than the previous conservative government. In response to my critique of his approach Smith argued in June 2014: "The way Mick Armstrong divides Syriza into 'non-revolutionary' (the leadership that has taken Syriza to where it is today) and an opposition that is baptised 'revolutionary' is a caricature."[126] Put to the test of practice on taking government, the utter capitulation of Tsipras and co. To the demands of big capital proved to be not a caricature, but rather a textbook case of reformist betrayal.

Smith fudged the whole question of reformism versus revolutionary politics, arguing that in the current political circumstances it is not necessary to build clear-cut revolutionary parties because "the social democratic parties and to a very large extent the Communist parties are finished as vehicles for working class aspirations".[127]

It is true that in many Western countries the working class base of the mainstream social democratic parties has been seriously eroded over the last 20-30 years and in Greece, France and Italy support for the old reformist socialist parties has collapsed. Nonetheless Smith's virtual dismissal of the influence of organised reformism on the Western working class is seriously mistaken.

Organised reformism is not simply based on parties like the ALP, but even more importantly on the trade union bureaucracy. And while in many countries the unions have been weakened, they still have an enormous impact on working class consciousness. In the Australian case this continuing influence was dramatically confirmed by the deep resonance for the union campaign against the Howard government's WorkChoices legislation and more recently the prominent role played by the unions, especially in Victoria, in the Equal Marriage plebiscite campaign. Moreover the rise, seemingly out of nowhere, of radical left winger Jeremy Corbyn to the leadership of the British Labour Party, arguably the most reactionary of all the old social democratic parties, is a dramatic reminder of the capacity of reformist parties to refurbish their image and regalvanise popular support.

In any case the roots of reformism in working class consciousness go well beyond its embodiment in reformist parties and union bureaucracies. The very nature of working class life – of having to go to work and be dominated by a boss – induces feelings of powerlessness and subservience. It opens the space for pro-capitalist ideas to have an influence. On the other hand the experience of exploitation and oppression also provokes resistance.

Working class consciousness is marked by a constant tension between a resigned acceptance of the system and ideas that partially reject capitalism. Whether or not there is an organised reformist party, most workers, most of the time, will be influenced by reformist ideas. The task of revolutionaries is to build on the elements of rebellion in workers' consciousness and try to win the most class conscious workers to a socialist standpoint. But that involves an ongoing battle against reformist *ideas*. Building an organisation that fudges these questions, that does not take a clear stand against reformist ideas, will in no way aid the revolutionary cause. It will at best lead to disorientation, at worst it will help create an obstacle to revolutionary advance.

We have seen this movie before. The idea of building all encompassing socialist parties which combine revolutionaries and reformists as an alternative to building a revolutionary organisation is simply a reversion to the approach of the Second Socialist International. It ended in disaster. Under the test of war the reformists abandoned any commitment to the defence of the most basic democratic rights and sent workers off to die in their millions in the trenches of World War I. When the revolutionaries objected, their reformist "comrades" combined with the extreme right to arrest or murder them.

But we don't have to go back to the history of the Second International to see the disastrous consequences of substituting a broad party for a revolutionary organisation. There are numerous more recent examples. One graphic case is that of Communist Refoundation in Italy which Smith held up as a model:

> Rifondazione ... has chosen an anti-capitalist and anti-Stalinist road.

> It is this party [Rifondazione], broad, heterogeneous and pluralist, which is behind most of the big mobilisations in Italy. It also works within broad united fronts. So the choice, either in Italy or in Scotland, is not between a narrow revolutionary organisation working through united fronts and a broad socialist party which doesn't.[128]

Originally formed as a left-wing split from the rightward moving Italian Communist Party, Refoundation also attracted the support of sections of the Italian far left. In the early 2000s Refoundation shifted leftwards and played an important role in leading mass anti-capitalist protests. However, the leftward jag was short-lived and Refoundation moved back towards accommodation with free market reformist forces. Refoundation then joined the centre-left coalition government which determinedly implemented neo-liberal policies. The result was betrayal after betrayal of working class interests, including voting to send Italian troops to Afghanistan and Lebanon.

But Refoundation in Italy was far from being the only disaster for this approach. In Brazil the Workers Party, which carried the hopes of many socialists in the 1990s, in government proved to be just as committed to neo-liberal policies and an alliance with US imperialism as its conservative rivals. In New Zealand the Alliance Party, which formed in 1991 following a left split from the Labour Party, collapsed in disarray after its most prominent leader Jim Anderton took a ministerial post in the Labour government. Murray Smith held great hopes for his own Scottish Socialist Party:

> the SSP is a party that corresponds to the challenges of the present period ... the SSP is the type of party that needs to be built today, rather than the old far left model.[129]

It fared little better. After first moving in the direction of Scottish nationalism, it then became embroiled in a bitter, largely apolitical internal dispute which led to a serious split. In the subsequent Scottish elections the vote of the rump SSP collapsed and it lost all its members of parliament. More recently of course there was the example of

Syriza which was elected to office in 2015 promising to reverse the vicious austerity measures imposed on Greek workers. But far from reversing austerity the Syriza Prime Minister Alexis Tsipras refused to put up even the semblance of a fight against the Greek and wider European establishments and ended up imposing an even more draconian austerity memorandum than the previous reformist (PASOK) and conservative governments. Syriza's betrayal had a devastating impact on the morale of the Greek left and the broader working class movement.

Meanwhile Podemos in Spain far from building an inspiring example of a new open democratic left wing party has been dominated by a small clique of media personalities who have run it in a thoroughly top down authoritarian manner. Everything has been subordinated to electoral success and consequently Podemos' opposition to austerity has been progressively watered down in a vain attempt to attract the votes of the supposed middle ground. Similarly the Podemos leadership capitulated to reactionary Spanish nationalism by refusing to take a forthright stance in support of the basic right for national self-determination for Catalonia. Closer to home the Australian Socialist Alliance, which some sections of the left, such as the Democratic Socialist Party (DSP), hoped would lay the basis for a broad socialist party here, utterly failed to make headway.

The clear conclusion must be that the argument that clear cut disciplined Marxist organisations are no longer needed and that socialists instead should concentrate all their energies on building broad socialists parties is at best a diversion, at worst a disaster. It is merely another opportunist short cut to break out of the isolation that socialists have faced since the last great upsurge of radicalism in the late 1960s and early 1970s. It is a short-cut that determined revolutionaries have to turn their face hard against.

This does not mean that if left reformist or centrist parties with serious working class support emerge Marxists should not actively participate in building them. Far from it. Any such development in Australia would be a very positive step forward. Such parties may well provide important opportunities for Marxists to begin to lay the basis for a genuine revolutionary party with roots in a section of the working class.

The approach of revolutionaries participating in them needs to be to consistently push forward the class struggle and argue in a non-sectarian fashion for principled left wing politics. In particular Marxists active in such broad parties need to stand firmly and publicly against any betrayals of working class interests by the reformist/centrist leadership. The goal must be winning the forces needed to create a genuinely revolutionary party, not seeing a broad socialist party as a substitute for a revolutionary party.

Revolutionaries need to intervene in such parties as *organised* revolutionary tendencies with their own publications and meetings, arguing a clear alternative road forward to that of the reformist or centrist leadership. The success of such an intervention could well depend on whether revolutionaries have previously built a cohesive propaganda group capable of such work.

A positive example of how Marxists should intervene in broad left parties like Syriza was provided by the Internationalist Workers Left (DEA) in Greece. DEA worked in a co-operative and non-sectarian fashion with a variety of other left wing political currents to help build Syriza. DEA operated openly as an organisation inside Syriza with its own publications, meetings, conferences, website, leadership bodies and so on. Despite coming under intense pressure from the Tsipras leadership it refused to dissolve its organisation. This was a vitally important decision.

Precisely because DEA operated as a disciplined and coherent revolutionary force inside Syriza it did not waver in its opposition to Tspiras' right wing course both before and after taking government. Nor did DEA confine its criticisms of Tspiras' backsliding to internal party forums but sought to mobilise the broader left and working class movement to oppose them on the streets and in the workplaces. The DEA-aligned MPs were the first to openly oppose and vote against in parliament Syriza's austerity memorandum and played an important role in rallying resistance by the other left forces in Syriza. In the face of the concerted left resistance within Syriza which was having a resonance in the working class movement Tspiras effectively blew Syriza apart. Subsequently DEA went on to help found a new anti-austerity party, Popular Unity.[130]

Hal Draper's alternative

There is another current of opinion that proclaims the need for a genuine revolutionary party and rejects the idea that a looser broad party can substitute for one, but argues that it is impossible to build a revolutionary party via the route of a propaganda group. One articulate representative of this standpoint is Hal Draper, a long-time Marxist writer and activist with politics similar to the tradition on which Socialist Alternative is based.

In his pamphlet *Toward a new beginning – on another road: The alternative to the micro-sect*, Draper dismisses a propaganda group as simply being a sect with only the negative connotations typically associated with the term. He argues: "To Marx, any organisation was a sect if it set up any special set of view...as its *organisational boundary*; if it made this special set of views the determinant of its organisational form." Draper goes on to claim: "There is no revolutionary mass party, or even semi-revolutionary mass party, which ever became a mass party by the road of the sect."[131]

In previous chapters I have outlined just a few of the numerous cases of mass socialist parties which were built from small propaganda groups. There are a host of others – virtually all of the early socialist parties in Eastern Europe, Communist parties all over Asia and the Middle East and the Trotskyists in Ceylon in the 1930s and 1940s. The example of Poland which I examined in chapter 5 is clear-cut and typical. But Draper simply denies reality, declaring: "her [Rosa Luxemburg's] Polish comrades established a sect, not a class party."[132] All I can say is that if an organisation of 40,000 members with a mass base in the working class and which played a leading role in the 1905 revolution is a sect then hasten the day that we have such a sect in Australia!

The Bolsheviks, according to Draper, were never a sect and never a membership organisation. They were simply a political centre cohered around a paper within a broader party. What Lenin called for, according to Draper, "was an all-inclusive socialist party in which the revolutionary Marxist center would constitute one tendency, hopefully eventually dominant."[133]

Draper's position simply does not hold water. He conveniently avoids any mention of the role of the Emancipation of Labour Group – a classic propaganda group, if ever there was one – in laying the basis for the Bolshevik Party. But in any case, after the defeat of the 1905 revolution a period of extreme reaction set in. Tens of thousands of activists were arrested, exiled or abandoned politics. The Bolsheviks were reduced to a tiny rump that did indeed set a sharp organisational boundary based on a set of ideas. For example they expelled the ultraleft Bogdanov group – one hallmark of a clearly defined propaganda group. The ultralefts in turn formed their own organised faction to fight the Bolsheviks.

By 1910 the number of Bolsheviks had declined to just a few hundred from 40,000 in 1907. "Membership in the Moscow district organization, which was as high as 500 toward the end of 1908, dropped to 250 in the middle of the following year and half a year later to 150; in 1910 the organization ceased to exist."[134] According to Schapiro, in 1909 the Bolsheviks had only five or six local committees left in the whole of Russia.[135] The remaining Bolsheviks had to fight to hold the line against the resurgence of strong right wing liquidationist currents on the one hand who opposed building a cohered underground organisation and on the other hand ultra leftist currents which refused to retreat in good order. The Mensheviks condemned the Bolsheviks as a pathetic "sect". "All of present-day development" wrote the Menshevik leader Martov "renders the formation of any kind of durable party-sect a pathetic reactionary utopia."[136] According to Geoffrey Swain, Lenin's support,

> was confined almost entirely to the Paris-based "circle for the support of the Workers' Newspaper". In this group there were some twenty-five to thirty members, but only five of those thirty were true Leninists...Apart from these, he was forced to rely on a small group of devoted supporters...The majority of émigré Bolsheviks had deserted Lenin and become conciliators.[137]

While Trotsky states:

> In 1910 in the whole country there were a few dozen people [in the Bolshevik party]. Some were in Siberia. But they were not organised. The people whom Lenin could reach by correspondence or by agent numbered about thirty or forty at most.[138]

Without getting into a pedantic and hair-splitting argument about what exactly is or is not a propaganda group, this sounds like a pretty close approximation to one. Much of the energy of the Bolshevik core around Lenin was spent on the vital task of political clarification and bitter polemics with Mensheviks, Bolshevik conciliators, ultraleft former Bolsheviks and all sorts of confused intermediary groups such as the conciliators grouped around Trotsky. At best Lenin and his supporters could win over individuals and train a cadre. In this context, even organising a tiny educational school for Bolshevik cadre abroad was an achievement. There was no party in any meaningful sense. When the level of struggle began to revive from about 1911 the Leninist propaganda core had to rebuild the Bolshevik faction in most parts of Russia from scratch.

Draper states that "there is no proposal for a sect form of organization in [Lenin's pamphlet] *What Is To Be Done*"[139] Of course not, because the whole point that Lenin was making in *What Is To Be Done*, which was published at the start of 1902 just 18 months before the Congress which founded the Russian Social Democratic Labour Party, was that the socialist movement had gone well beyond the stage of local circle organisation. A revolutionary party organised around a nation-wide newspaper was immediately on the agenda. Thus Lenin wrote: "Give us an organisation of revolutionaries, and we will overturn Russia." And later:

> The organisation, which will form round this newspaper...will be ready for everything, from upholding the honour, the prestige, and the continuity of the Party in periods of acute revolutionary "depression" to preparing for, appointing the time for, and carrying out the nation-wide armed uprising.[140]

Draper argues that:

> The membership organization to which Lenin looked was to be a mass party, not one consisting exclusively of those who agreed with his revolutionary Marxism, but rather a mass party broad enough to include all socialists, indeed all militant workers. It would have different tendencies within it, and the consistent marxists might be a minority at least for a while.

> It was the Mensheviks and right-wingers, not Lenin, who split rather than permit a left-wing majority. Nor, in the years of the Bolshevik party's formation, did Lenin make a virtue out of necessity: he did not adopt the view the Party had to be limited to Bolsheviks. On the contrary, he fought consistently for the conception of a broad Party, in which, however, the left wing had as much right to take over the leadership by a democratic vote as did the right wing.[141]

This had been Lenin's attitude at the time of the 1903 split and for some years afterwards. But Lenin's approach was to shift markedly away from this orthodox social democratic position, and he came to see the need for a party that consisted only of revolutionary Marxists. 1912 saw the formal foundation of an overwhelmingly Bolshevik dominated party completely separate party from the Mensheviks.[142] This was "an advance on Lenin's own earlier position, in that the 1903 split had in large part been the work of the Mensheviks, and Lenin had frequently been willing to countenance reunification, whereas now he broke with the Mensheviks once and for all."[143]

In 1912 the Bolsheviks ran candidates in opposition to the Mensheviks in the elections for the Tsarist Duma. In 1913, at Lenin's urging, the Bolshevik Duma deputies split from the Mensheviks to form an independent fraction. The Bolsheviks stood their own candidates in union elections. By June 1914 the Bolsheviks controlled 14 of the 18 unions in Petersburg and ten of the 13 in Moscow.[144]

Draper further claims that:

> Nor were these factions (Bolshevik as well as Menshevik) "membership organizations" in the sense of the sects we have been trying to build...the membership organizations in Russia were local and regional party groups which might be part Bolshevik and part Menshevik in sympathy...

> Both the Bolsheviks and the Mensheviks were, in organizational form, not membership sects, and not even "factions" in any organizational meaning relevant to today. What were they? Both were political centers based on a propaganda/publishing enterprise, plus a central organizational apparatus for forging links with sections of the workers' movement, through "agents", literary collaborators, etc.[145]

This is nonsense. It is true that both the Bolsheviks and Mensheviks had organised centres that elaborated a political line and published papers, journals and so on. But this should be a key element of any half serious revolutionary party or propaganda group. It is also true that Lenin's faction was not the authoritarian monolith of Stalinist myth. For a long time it was relatively fluid, informal and messy. In many of the dispersed party groups in the regional centres of the Tsarist Empire, there was not a sharp separation between the supporters of the Bolsheviks and the Mensheviks. Nonetheless there were organised Bolshevik and Menshevik factions with formal memberships. They were not just some vague political centre. Trotsky described the situation at the 1907 London Congress of the Russian Social Democratic Party:

> Each of the factions and national organizations met separately during recesses between official sessions, worked out its own line of conduct and designated its own speakers...At the final session of the Bolshevik faction, after the closing of the Congress, a secret Bolshevik Center was elected...composed of fifteen members.[146]

The Bolsheviks held their own congresses – the first in Finland in December 1905 – and elected their own Central Committee. Three conferences of Bolshevik local committees were held as early as September-December 1904. By the time of the 1905 revolution the Bolsheviks had established their own Committees in Petersburg, Moscow and other centres such as Odessa, Baku, Batum and Tiflis. During the course of the 1905 revolution the Bolsheviks established their own factory cells independent of the Mensheviks – almost 100 in Petersburg and 40 in Moscow.

> By the fourth Congress in April 1906, membership had grown, it is estimated, to 13,000 for the Bolsheviks and 18,000 for the Mensheviks. Another estimate (for October 1906) was 33,000 Bolsheviks, 43,000 Mensheviks...By 1907 the total membership had increased to

150,000: Bolsheviks – 46,143, Mensheviks – 38,174, Bund – 25,468, and the Polish and Latvian parts of the party 25,654 and 13,000 respectively.[147]

The war drew a sharp line

Draper omits any reference to the dramatic impact that World War I had on Lenin's whole political outlook, in particular Lenin's development of his theory of imperialism. The outbreak of war had blown out of the water any idea that you could have a broad inclusive party containing revolutionaries and reformists, even left-wing reformists. This was a vital issue that Lenin had to face up to in his analysis of the era of imperialism. Lenin's theory of imperialism entailed not just an economic analysis of this latest stage of capitalism, but, as Georg Lukacs puts it, also "a theory of the different currents within the working-class movement in the age of imperialism."[148] As early as November 1914 the Bolshevik Central Committee had issued the slogan "Long live a proletarian International freed from opportunism."[149] In his pamphlet *Socialism and War* written in 1915 Lenin declared:

> We are firmly convinced that, in the present state of affairs, a split with the opportunists and chauvinists is the prime duty of revolutionaries...our Party will work indefatigably in the above-mentioned direction...and through its day-by-day activities will build up the Russian section of the Marxist International.[150]

The right wing of Social Democracy openly backed the imperialist war and commonly entered into governments that sent millions of workers to their deaths in defence of the profits of the capitalists. The so-called Social Democratic centre looked to pacifist solutions but refused to actually fight the war. So the centrists too ended up supporting the imperialist system. The fight with opportunism was not some "sectarian" squabble, not a mere difference of opinion among socialists which could be settled by comradely debate within a united party. It was not a dispute over the best strategies and tactics to achieve a shared goal of socialism. This meant for Lenin that there had to be a sharp split in the international working class movement between revolutionaries on the one side and reformists and centrists of all shades on the other. As Georg Lukacs put it:

> ...opportunism is the class enemy of the proletariat within its own camp. The removal of the opportunists from the labour movement is therefore the first, essential prerequisite of the successful start of the struggle against the bourgeoisie.[151]

The new Third International which Lenin campaigned for "was to be precisely an instrument of war – international civil war against the imperialist bourgeoisie – and therefore could tolerate in its ranks neither a fifth column nor waverers."[152]

Of course the fact that Lenin's Bolshevik party was built on the back of a propaganda group, Plekhanov's Emancipation of Labour Group, and that after the defeat of the 1905 revolution the Bolsheviks had to rebuild again from a small propaganda core does not prove that the *only* road to a revolutionary party is via a propaganda group. We have no crystal ball. If other opportunities arise, then Marxists need to grasp them. But we have to begin somewhere, and we have to optimise the use of the resources we actually possess. In the concrete circumstances facing Marxists in Australia and many other countries today, where there are at best a few hundred or a thousand or so active revolutionaries, we face no alternative but starting from the base of a socialist propaganda group.

No better option is on offer.

There are no short cuts to mass influence. For tiny socialist groups the idea that if they set up a looser, politically softer formation that demands less active commitment from its members they could somehow break out and win widespread working class support is wishful thinking – and dangerous wishful thinking at that. It points away from where revolutionaries need to go.

The alternative that Hal Draper puts forward is one of a political centre "based on a propaganda/publishing enterprise, plus a central organizational apparatus for forging links with sections of the workers' movement, through 'agents', literary collaborators, etc."[153] How this would radically differ from a propaganda group is not at all clear. The "agents" of the political centre seem remarkably similar to the cadres of a propaganda group.

The advantages Draper claims for his model are extremely dubious to say the least. He argues that "a political center can undertake a relationship with its followers which is not bedevilled by the rigid requirements of organizational life, its life-and-death votes, faction fights, splits, internal disputes" which are the hallmarks of a propaganda group/ sect.[154] But in Draper's model the core members of the political centre are a totally self-selecting group, effectively a clique, which is not subject to any democratic control or accountability. In contrast a vibrant propaganda group thrives on democratic debate and accountability. The "votes" and "internal disputes" that Draper disparages are a vital mechanism by which the activists can have an impact on the political direction of the organisation. In any case even a cursory examination of the history of the Bolsheviks, which Draper upholds as a supposed model of his "political centre", shows that they were repeatedly wracked by all of these phenomena.

That, however, is not the main point. Draper's schema effectively downplays the importance of revolutionaries clarifying their ideas and drawing sharp lines of demarcation, i.e. organisational conclusions, from them. The "life-and-death votes, faction fights, splits, internal disputes" that Draper so decries are not some terrible "sectarian" excess of small socialist groups. They are an inevitable and necessary element in the building of a mass revolutionary party. This is not to glorify splits and faction fights. There have been plenty of totally unnecessary and badly handled faction fights, and small groups are prone to split over secondary issues.

Nonetheless, no genuine working class party, whether it be the Russian Bolsheviks or the German Social Democrats, has ever developed without them. For in the real world of politics, whatever the organisational form, there will be disagreements in any organisation that is not totally lifeless. If these disagreements are not clarified and debated out, then as axiomatically as night follows day, confused or opportunist ideas will win out. Furthermore, no matter how loose a socialist organisation is, in less revolutionary periods more conservative and reformist forces will be likely to refuse to work co-operatively with revolutionaries in the same organisation, if the revolutionaries seriously try to clarify the issues in dispute.

Conclusion

Unfortunately there are no guarantees in politics. The task of building a revolutionary party is far from simple and straightforward. Plenty of small socialist groups have gone off the rails well before they have come anywhere near to establishing a revolutionary party. However, for socialists who are committed to fighting to change the world, there is no alternative but to organise the forces that do currently exist. And if there are only twenty of you, or two hundred, or even two thousand, that means recognising the fact that at this stage of your development you need to see yourself as a propaganda group. Facing up to what you are, not kidding yourself, not pretending you are something broader or more influential is the first step towards building on a sound basis. Being clear on what you are and on the tasks confronting a propaganda group opens up the possibility of genuine growth and at some point, when there are sharp shifts in the political climate, of a qualitative breakthrough which can lay the basis for a mass revolutionary party.

This is not some dream or utopian schema. The experience of history is that time and time again small groups of revolutionaries armed with a burning commitment to Marxist politics and a fierce determination to build have been able to break through and establish parties that could play a leading role in struggles for workers' rights and even lead a challenge for power. That is the lesson of Plekhanov's pioneering work, of Poland at the start of the twentieth century, of the Chinese revolutionaries in the 1920s and of the Vietnamese Trotskyists in the 1930s and 1940s. In the last great radical upsurge in the 1960s and 1970s a similar pattern began to occur in country after country as tiny groups of largely student revolutionaries attempted with some limited success to break the hold of the Stalinist Communist parties over the most advanced sections of the working class.

The collapse of the Stalinist regimes in Eastern Europe and Russia removed an obscene obstacle that blocked the path of genuine revolutionary Marxism for over fifty years. However in the immediate aftermath the ideologues of capitalism used the demise of those authoritarian regimes as a justification for their argument that there was simply no alternative to the existing capitalist order. In the wake of the devastation wreaked on country after country by the 2007/2008 global financial crisis, the endless series of murderous imperialist wars and the growth of the far right internationally the argument to bow down before the status quo has begun to wear terribly thin. This provides socialists with both an opportunity and a challenge. We now have the responsibility of making Marxism relevant to a new generation of fighters and laying the basis for a movement that can fire the hopes and imagination of tens of millions of people appalled by the horrors of twenty-first century capitalism.

Bibliography

Alexander, Robert 1991, *International Trotskyism 1929-1985: A Documented Analysis of the Movement*, Duke University.

Armstrong, Mick 2001, *1,2,3, What Are We Fighting For? The Australian student movement from its origins to the 1970s*, Socialist Alternative.

Armstrong, Mick 2006, *The I.W.W. in Australia*, Socialist Alternative.

Armstrong, Mick and Tom Bramble 2007, *The Labor Party: A Marxist Analysis*, Socialist Alternative.

Armstrong, Mick 2010 "The origins of Socialist Alternative: summing up the debate", *Marxist Left Review*, 1, Spring.

Armstrong, Mick 2014, "A critique of the writings of Murray Smith on broad left parties", *Marxist Left Review*, 7, Summer.

Armstrong, Mick 2016, "The broad left party question after Syriza", *Marxist Left Review*, 11, Summer.

Arnove, Anthony, Peter Binns, Tony Cliff, Chris Harman, Ahmed Shawki 2003, *Russia: From Workers' State to State Capitalism*, Haymarket.

Baron, Samuel H. 1963, *Plekhanov: The Father of Russian Marxism*, Stanford University Press.

Birchall, Ian 1981, *The smallest mass party in the world. Building the Socialist Workers Party, 1951-1979*, SWP.

Birchall, Ian 2011, *Tony Cliff. A Marxist for His Time*, Bookmarks.

Blit, Lucjan 1971, *The Origins of Polish Socialism. The History and Ideas of the First Polish Socialist Party 1878-1886*, Cambridge University Press.

Blobaum, Robert 1984, *Feliks Dzierzynski and the SDKPil: A Study in the Origins of Polish Communism*, Columbia University Press.

Blobaum, Robert 1995, *Revolujca, Russian Poland, 1904-1907*, Cornell University Press.

Bramble, Tom 1998, *War on the waterfront*, Brisbane Defend Our Unions Committee.

Bramble, Tom 2015, *Introducing Marxism: A theory of Social Change*, A Socialist Alternative publication.

Bramble, Tom and Rick Kuhn 2011, *Labor's Conflict. Big business, workers and the politics of class*, Cambridge University Press.

Callinicos, Alex 1990, *Trotskyism*, Open University Press.

Cliff , Tony 1957, "Perspectives on the Permanent Arms Economy", *Socialist Review*, May 1957.

Cliff, Tony 1982, *Neither Washington nor Moscow. Essays on revolutionary socialism*, Bookmarks.

Cliff, Tony 1984, *Building small groups*, International Socialists.

Cliff, Tony 1986, *Lenin: Building the Party 1893-1914*, Bookmarks.

Cliff, Tony 1987, "55 years a Revolutionary", *Socialist Review*, July/August 1987.

Cliff, Tony 1988, *State capitalism in Russia*, Bookmarks.

Cliff, Tony 2000, *A world to win. Life of a revolutionary*, Bookmarks.

Cliff, Tony, Duncan Hallas, Chris Harman, Leon Trotsky 2003, *Party and Class*, Haymarket.

Collins, Henry and Chimen Abramsky1965, *Karl Marx and the British Labour Movement: Years of the first International*, Macmillan.

Colombo, Yurii 2002, "The Italian left in the 1970s", *International Socialist Review*, No 26.

De Lucia, Michael 1971, *The Remaking of French Syndicalism, 1911-1918: The Growth of the Reformist Philosophy*, PhD Brown University.

Dirlik, Arif 1989, *The Origins of Chinese Communism*, Oxford University Press.

Draper Hal (ed) 1970, *The Permanent Arms Economy*.

Draper, Hal 1971, *Toward a New Beginning – On Another Road: The Alternative to the Micro-Sect*. www.marxists.org/archive/draper/workers/1971/alt/alt.htm.

Draper, Hal 1973, *Anatomy of the Micro-Sect*, www.marxists.org/archive/draper/1973/xx/microsect.htm.

Founding of the First International, 1937, International Publishers.

Fraser, Ronald (ed) 1988, *1968: A Student Generation in Revolt*, Pantheon.

Gaspar, Phil (ed) 2005, *The Communist Manifesto: A Road Map to History's Most Important Political Document*, Haymarket.

Ginsborg, Paul 1990, *A History of Contemporary Italy – Society and Politics 1943-1988*, Penguin Books.

Goldner, Loren 1997, "The Anti-Colonial Movement in Vietnam", *New Politics*, Vol 6, No 3 (new series), whole No 23.

Hallas, Duncan 1985, *The Comintern*, Bookmarks.

Hallas, Duncan 2003, *Trotsky's Marxism and other essays*, Haymarket.

Haimson, Leopold 1955, *The Russian Marxists and the Origins of Bolshevism*, Harvard University Press.

Harman, Chris 1982, *The Lost Revolution*, Bookmarks.

Harman, Chris 1984, *Explaining the Crisis*, Bookmarks.

Harman, Chris 1988, *The Fire Last Time: 1968 and after*, Bookmarks.

Harman, Chris 1991, *The Revolutionary Paper*, A Socialist Workers Party pamphlet.

Harris, Nigel 1978, *The Mandate of Heaven. Marx and Mao in Modern China*, Quartet.

Hassan, Omar 2016, "Podemos and left populism", *Marxist Left Review*, 11, Summer.

Hemery, Daniel 1990, "La Lutte and the Vietnamese Trotskyists", *Revolutionary History*, Volume 3, No 2.

Hose, Allyson 2012, *The Baiada poultry workers' strike – How class struggle unionism can win*, Socialist Alternative.

Isaacs, Harold R 1961, *The Tragedy of the Chinese Revolution*, Stanford University Press.

Judge, Cecilia and Adam Bottomley 2012, "Still fighting for equal pay", *Marxist Left Review*, 4, Summer.

Kemp, Tom 1984, *Stalinism in France*, New Park.

Kidron, Michael 1970, *Western Capitalism Since the War*, Penguin.

Kidron, Michael 1974, *Capitalism and Theory*, Pluto Press.

Kit-ching, Chan Lau 1999, *From Nothing to Nothing. The Chinese Communist Movement and Hong Kong 1921-1936*, Hurst & Company.

Lane, David 1968, *The Roots of Russian Communism*, Pennsylvania State University Press.

Le Blanc, Paul 2012, *The birth of the Bolshevik party in 1912*, http://links.org.au/node/2832.

Lenin, V.I. 1961, *What Is To Be Done*, *Collected Works*, Vol 5, Progress Publishers.

Lenin, V.I. 1962, *Collected Works*, Vol 10, Progress Publishers.

Lenin, V.I. 1964, *Collected Works*, Vol 21, Progress Publishers.

Lukacs, Georg 1977, *Lenin: A Study in the Unity of his Thought*, New Left Books.

Lumley, Robert 1990, *States of Emergency. Cultures of revolt in Italy from 1968 to 1978*, Verso.

Marco, Nini 1977, "Italy", *International Discussion Bulletin*, No 4, SWP.

Marx, Karl 1972, *Theses on Feuerbach* in K Marx, F Engels, V Lenin, *On Historical Materialism*, Progress Publishers.

Marx, Karl 1973, *The Revolutions of 1848*, Penguin.

Marx, Karl and Frederick Engels 1973, "Address of the Central Committee to the Communist League (March 1850)" in Marx, Karl, *The Revolutions of 1848*, Penguin.

Meisner, Maurice 1974, *Li Ta-Chao and the Origins of Chinese Marxism*, Atheneum.

Molyneux, John 2003, *Marxism and the Party*, Haymarket.

Molyneux, John 2012, *Anarchism: A Marxist Criticism*, Bookmarks.

Naimark, Norman 1979, *The History of the "Proletariat": The Emergence of Marxism in the Kingdom of Poland, 1870-1887*, East European Quarterly.

Naimark, Norman 1983, *Terrorists and Social Democrats. The Russian Revolutionary Movement Under Alexander III*, Harvard University Press.

Nettl, Peter 1969, *Rosa Luxemburg*, Oxford University Press.

Nimitz, August H 2000, *Marx and Engels: Their Contribution to the Democratic Breakthrough*, State University of New York Press.

Oakley, Corey 2013, "What kind of organisation do socialists need?", *Marxist Left Review*, 5, Summer.

O'Shea, Louise 2011, "The campaign for equal marriage rights", *Marxist Left Review*, 2011, Autumn.

Offord, Derek 1986, *The Russian revolutionary movement in the 1880s*, Cambridge University Press.

The Origins of the International Socialists, Pluto Press, 1971.

Pirani, Simon 1987, *Vietnam and Trotskyism*, Communist League (Australia).

Plekhanov, G. 1961, *Selected Philosophical Works*, Vol 1, Foreign Languages Publishing House.

Potter, Tim 2001, "The end of terror" in *Genoa: la lotta continua*, Socialist Worker pamphlet.

Red Notes 1978, *Italy 1977-8: Living With An Earthquake*.

Ridley, F 1970, *Revolutionary Syndicalism in France*, Cambridge University Press.

Saich, Tony, *The Chinese Communist Party during the era of the Comintern (1919-1943)*. Article prepared for Juergen Rojahn, "Comintern and National Communist Parties Project", International Institute of Social History.

Sacks, Milton 1959, "Marxism in Viet Nam", in Frank N Trager (Ed), *Marxism in South-East Asia: A Study of Four Countries*, Stanford University Press.

Schapiro, Leonard 1971, *The Communist Party of the Soviet Union*, Vintage.

Sharpe, John 1973, *Stalinism and Trotskyism in Vietnam*, A Spartacist Pamphlet.

Smith, Murray 2002, "Where is the SWP going?" *International Socialism Journal*, 97.

Smith, Murray 2003, "The broad party, the revolutionary party and the united front: a reply to John Rees", *International Socialism Journal*, 100.

Smith, Murray 2014, "Broad left parties: Murray Smith replies to Socialist Alternative's Mick Armstrong", http://links.org.au/node/3919.

Smith, S.A. 2000, *A Road is Made. Communism in Shanghai 1920-1927*, University of Hawai'i Press.

Swain, Geoffrey 1983, *Russian Social Democracy and the Legal Labour Movement 1906-14*, Macmillan.

The Origins of the International Socialists, 1971, Pluto Press.

Trotsky, Leon 1967, *Stalin*, Stein and Day.

Trotsky, Leon 1974 *Writings 1938-39*, Pathfinder.

Van, Ngo 1995, *Revolutionaries They Could Not Break. The Fight for the Fourth International in Indochina 1930-1945*, Index Books.

Vance, T.N. 2008, *The Permanent War Economy*, Centre for Socialist History.

Widgery, David 1976, *The Left in Britain 1956-1968*, Penguin.

Wilkin, Phil 1980, *The Relationship between the Communist and Socialist Parties in France 1921-1924*, PhD Indiana University.

Wohl, Robert 1966, *French Communism in the Making, 1914-1924*, Stanford University Press.

Woods, Alan 1999, *Bolshevism: The road to revolution*, Wellred.

Endnotes

Introduction

1   For a comprehensive introduction to Marxist politics see Bramble 2015.

Chapter 1 – The nature and tasks of a socialist propaganda group

2   O'Shea 2011.

3   Judge and Bottomley 2012.

4   Bramble 1998, Hose 2012.

5   https://redflag.org.au/article/unity-and-organisation-left and Oakley 2013.

6   Lenin, 1978, p31.

7   See Armstrong 2001.

Chapter 2 – Karl Marx and Frederick Engels: revolutionary activists and party builders

8   Marx 1972, p13.

9   Nimitz 2000, pix.

10   Nimitz 2000, p2.

11   Nimitz 2000, p1.

12   See Draper 1978.

13   Marx 1973, p323.

14   Collins and Abramsky 1965.

15   Founding of the First International 1937, p39.

16   Nimitz 2000, p272.

Chapter 3 – Plekhanov and the foundation of Marxism in Russia

17   Offord 1986, pp17-19.

18   Baron 1963, p19.

19   Haimson 1955, p34.

20   Woods 1999, p58.

21   Plekhanov 1961, p404. See also Blit 1971, p63.

22   The other important network for spreading Marxist literature in Russia in these years was that of the Polish Marxists.

23   For the development of the underground revolutionary movement in Russia see Naimark, 1983.

24   For Plekhanov's role in preparing the ground for Lenin see Cliff 1986.

25   Lenin 1962, p113.

Chapter 4 – The rise of Marxism in Poland

26   For the early history see Blit 1971.

27   The US Marxist Hal Draper argues that Rosa Luxemburg's "Polish comrades established a sect, not a class party." The SDKP was very much an organisation that in Draper's words made a "special set of views the determinant of its organisational form." Draper 1971, pp3-6. Yet the idea that the Polish Marxists built a sect is nonsense. Yes, they were sectarian on the national question and made numerous other errors. Nonetheless they played a decisive role in the 1905 revolution and built a party that had a stronger implantation in the working class than the Russian Bolsheviks. For further discussion of these issues see the later chapter: "Is there an easier road?"

28   Blobaum1984, p226.

29   Blobaum 1995, pp61-62.

30   Less than Socialist Alternative's membership in Melbourne in 2017, though Warsaw in the 1900s was a smaller city.

31   An important point to note in reply to Draper.

32   Blobaum 1995, pp195-96.

33   Blobaum 1995, p196.

34   Blobaum 1984, p174.

35   Blobaum 1984, p231.

Chapter 5 – Early French Communism

36   For the Comintern see Hallas 1985.

37   See De Lucia 1971 and also Ridley 1970.

38   See Harman, 1982.

39   Wohl 1966, p121.

40   Wohl 1966, p129.

41   Wohl 1966, p132.

42   Kemp 1984, p66.

43   Hallas 1985, p76.

44   Wilkin 1980.

Chapter 6 – The origins of Communism in China

45   Meisner 1974, p53.

46   Smith, S.A. 2000, p10.

47   Smith, S.A. 2000, p9.

48   Saich, p9.

49   S.A. Smith 2000, p10.

50   Dirlik 1989, pp253-254.

51   Saich, p11.

52   Dirlik 1989, p247.

53   Kit-ching 1999, p20.

54   Kit-ching 1999, p59.

55   See Isaacs 1961.

56   For the subsequent history see Harris 1978.

Chapter 7 – The Vietnamese Trotskyists: building an alternative to Stalinism

57   Van 1995, p51.

58   Van 1995, p19.

59   According to Robert Alexander there were three Trotskyist currents at this time: the Indochinese Communism group led by Thau, the Indochinese Left opposition led by Ho Huu Tuong and Dao Hung Long and a study circle, Editions de l'Opposition de Gauche, organised by Huynh van Phuong and Phan van Chanh, Alexander 1991, p3.

60   Van 1995, pp30-31.

61   Hemery 1990, p15.

62   Hemery 1990, p16.

63   Goldner 1997.

64   Van 1995, p47.

65   Hemery 1990, p16.

66   Van 1995, p51.

67   Alexander 1991, p10.

68   Pirani 1987, p31.

69   Van 1995, p59.

70   Sharpe 1973, p11.

71   Pirani 1987, p65.

72   Sharpe 1973, p21.

73   Sacks 1959, p156.

74   Sharpe 1973, p18-19.

Chapter 8 – The last upturn: Case No 1 – the revolutionary left in Italy

75   The Italian Hot Autumn of 1969 was the third largest strike movement in history in terms of total days on strike.

76   Colombo 2002, p57.

77   Agnelli was the boss of FIAT, Harman 1988, p142.

78   The Pisa students were strongly influenced by the workerists associated with the radical journal Quaderni Rossi, Lumley 1990, p65.

79   Fraser 1988, p182.

80   Ginsborg 1990, p309.

81   Students marched in large numbers in support of workers during the mass strikes of 1960 and 1963, Lumley1990, p25.

82   This is not to say that the PCI had no influence on campus. In 1964-65 the Unione Goliardica Italiana which grouped together supporters of the PCI and the Socialist Party (PSI) won an average 17 per cent of the vote in student elections. Many of the initial activists were formed within the PCI or the PSI left. But by the end of 1968 most student activists had broken with the PCI, Lumley 1990, p63-65.

83   Colombo 2002, p60 gives a figure of 8,000 at Lotta Continua's 1975 conference. While Red Notes 1978, p110, probably exaggeratedly claims: "At its peak, it had about 50,000 activists, 100 full-time paid officials, branch offices in all 94 Italian provinces and 21 neighborhood offices in Rome alone."

84   Harman 1988, p203.

85   Lotta Continua, 14 February 1970.

86   Harman 1988, p197.

87   Il Manifesto was a daily paper founded by a group of intellectuals that split from the PCI in 1969. Though more rightist than the other left groups it was also influenced by Maoism and spontaneism. It had a significant influence on the radical milieu. At its height in the early 1970s it had 20,000 members according to Marco 1977, p7.

88   Harman 1988, p206.

89   In 1977 it had 6,000 members according to Marco 1977, p8.

90   Harman 1988, p208.

91   Potter 2001, p28.

Chapter 9 – The last upturn: Case No 2 – the International Socialists in Britain

92   For the most comprehensive history of the IS/SWP see Birchall 2011. On the relationship between Socialist Alternative and the IST see Armstrong 2010.

93   https://www.ons.gov.uk/employmentandlabourmarket/peopleinwork/workplacedisputesandworkingconditions/articles/labourdisputes/latest.

94   The slogan was borrowed from the Shachtmanite Independent Socialist League in the USA, Birchall 2011, p136.

95   Cliff first elaborated his position in an RCP internal document in 1948. See The Origins of the International Socialists, 1971 and Cliff 1988.

96   Birchall 2011, p133.

97   See Cliff 1957, Kidron 1970, Kidron 1974, Harman 1984. The American Marxist TN Vance first advanced a theory of the Permanent War Economy in the 1940s and early 1950s see Draper 1970, Vance 2008.

98   Callinicos 1990, p82.

99   Birchall 1981, p5.

100   Cliff 2000, p208.

101   Cliff 1987, p17.

102   Birchall 1981, p5.

103   Cliff 1987, p16.

104   Birchall 1981, p6.

105   Cliff 2000, p67.

106   Birchall 1981, p7.

107   Cliff 2000, p77.

108   Birchall 1981, p8.

109   Birchall 1981, p9.

110   Birchall 1981, p14.

111   Cliff 1987, p18.

112   Harman 1988, p157.

113   Cliff 1982, pp218-238.

114   Callinicos 1990, pp84-85.

115   Harman 1988, p165.

116   Birchall 1981, p16.

117   Birchall 2011, p359.

118   Cliff 2000, p104. A tendency that Cliff himself was not immune from as Birchall
        notes, Birchall 2011, p344.

119   Callinicos 1990, p87.

120   Harman 1988, p276.

Chapter 10 – Is there an easier road?

121   I have not space here to deal with the arguments of anarchists and autonomists
        that oppose any form of party organisation. See Molyneux, 2003 and 2012 and
        Cliff, Hallas, Harman, Trotsky, 2003.

122   For the argument against the fruitless endeavour of socialists trying to influ-
        ence the ALP see Armstrong and Bramble 2007 and Bramble and
        Kuhn 2011.

123   For Syriza see Armstrong 2016 and for Podemos see Hassan 2016.

124   For a more detailed critique of Smith's writings see Armstrong 2014.

125   Smith, Murray 2002, p44.

126   Smith, Murray 2014.

127   Smith, Murray 2003, p69.

128   Smith, Murray 2003, p77.

129   Smith, Murray 2002, p45.

130   Armstrong 2016.

131   Draper 1971, p3, 12.

132   Draper 1971, p5.

133   Draper 1973, p8.

134   Trotsky 1967, p95.

135   Schapiro, 1971, p103.

136   Trotsky 1967, p111.

137   Swain 1983, p136.

138   Trotsky 1974, p257.

139   Draper 1971, p9.

140   Lenin 1961, pp467, 514-515.

141   Draper 1971, p10.

142   There has been much controversy in recent years as to whether the 1912 conference led to the formation of a separate Bolshevik party. See Le Blanc 2012 for an overview of the debate.

143   Molyneux 2003, p64.

144   Cliff 1975, pp331-332.

145   Draper 1971, p11.

146   Trotsky 1967, p91.

147   Lane 1968, pp12-13.

148   Lukacs 1977, p53.

149   Lenin 1964, p34.

150   Lenin 1964, pp 329-330.

151   Lukacs 1977, p58.

152   Molyneux 2003, p71.

153   Draper 1971, p11.

154   Draper 1973, p11.

This work was published by Red Flag Books, an Imprint of the revolutionary socialist organisation Socialist Alternative.

Red Flag Books offers hundreds of other titles covering Marxist politics, revolutionary history, and much more.

Browse our store at shop.redflag.org.au

Spreading the revolutionary ideas we need for a world in crisis.

REDFLAG

The newspaper of Socialist Alternative

Australia's #1 socialist publication relies on your support to continue.
Read now and subscribe.

redflag.org.au

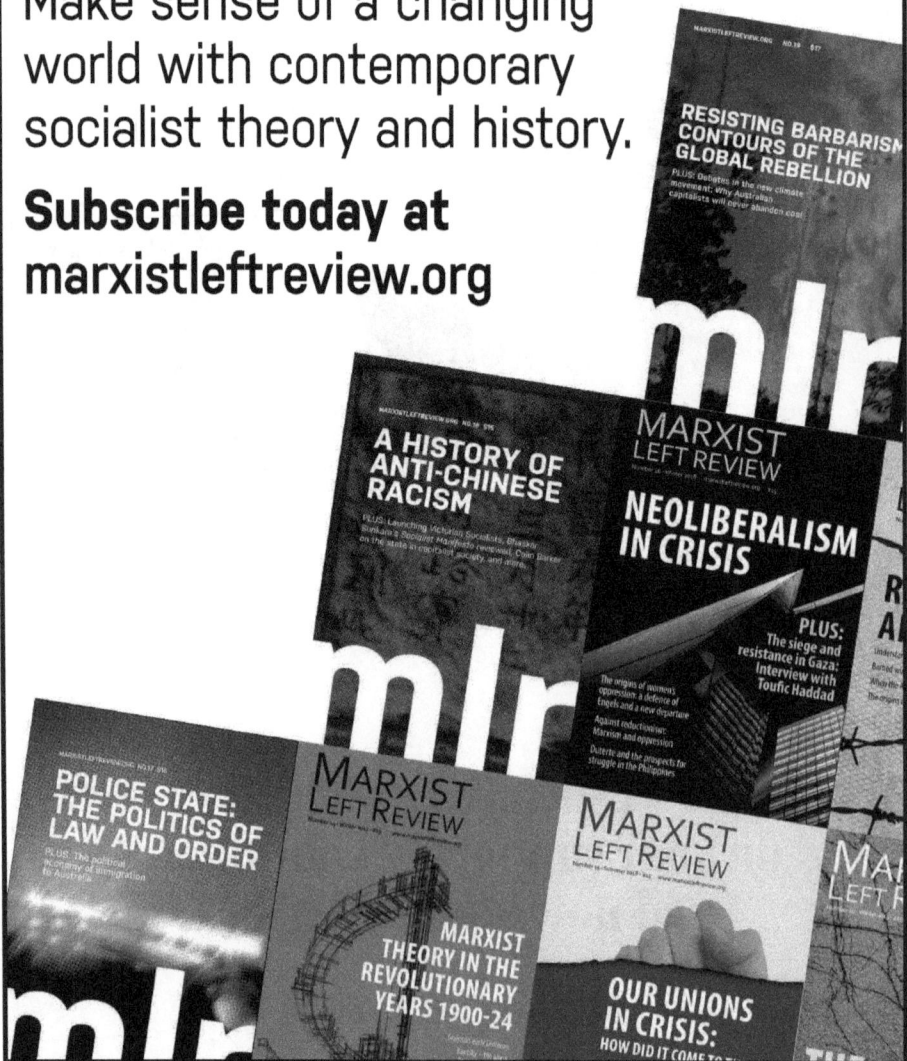

www.ingramcontent.com/pod-product-compliance
Lightning Source LLC
Chambersburg PA
CBHW022102020426
42335CB00012B/800